Telling Our Story

Recent Essays on Zionism,
the Middle East, and the Path to Peace

Einat Wilf

Edited by Ayelet Kahane and Batsheva Neuer

Copyright © 2018 Einat Wilf
All rights reserved.

Zionism has a story to tell that is not only about Jews or for Jews. Zionism has a story to tell that, when properly understood, has the power to inspire people and peoples to great acts of daring and sacrifice. Zionism tells a simple story: Victimhood is not destiny. A history of marginalization, humiliation, discrimination, persecution, massacres, and even genocide can be transcended. A people, no matter how downtrodden, can find within themselves the power to change their future.

The inspirational power of Zionism lay not only in its call to action, but in its vocabulary of human equality, liberty, and dignity. Zionism called upon the Jewish people to take action to achieve their rightful place among the nations as equals—nothing more, nothing less. This was a simple, but compelling, argument: In a world where nations and peoples were increasingly considered to possess a universal right to sovereignty in states of their own, where they could enjoy liberty and dignity, free from the oppressions of empire, the Jewish nation possessed that right as well.

The Tower
December 15, 2016

ABOUT THE AUTHOR

Dr. Einat Wilf is a leading intellectual and original thinker on matters of foreign policy, economics, education, and Israel and the Jewish people. A member of the Israeli Parliament from 2010-2013 on behalf of the Labor and Independence parties, she is considered one of Israel's most articulate representatives on the international stage.

Dr. Wilf has a BA in Government and Fine Arts from Harvard University, an MBA from INSEAD in France, and a PhD in Political Science from the University of Cambridge. Born and raised in Israel, Dr. Wilf served as an Intelligence Officer in the Israel Defense Forces.

Dr. Wilf's past experience includes service as Chair of the Education, Sports and Culture Committee, Chair of the Knesset Sub-Committee for Israel and the Jewish People, and Member of the influential Foreign Affairs and Defense Committee in the 18th Knesset. She served as the Baye Foundation Adjunct Fellow at the Washington Institute for Near East Policy, a Senior Fellow at the Jewish People Policy Institute, Foreign Policy Advisor to Vice Prime Minister Shimon Peres, and a strategic consultant with McKinsey & Company.

Dr. Wilf is the author of four books that explore key issues in Israeli society: "My Israel, Our Generation," about Israel's younger generation; "Back to Basics: How to Save Israeli Education (at no additional cost)"; "It's NOT the Electoral System, Stupid"; and "Winning the War of Words."

TABLE OF CONTENTS

I. TELLING OUR STORY

The right of the Jewish people to have a country in its own homeland is a universal right, which is reserved for every people – the right to stand on its own authority and to control its fate. As long as the world is divided into some 200 countries, on the basis of the principle of self-determination for peoples and nations, the Jewish people have a right to this. The Palestinian Arabs also have a right to self-determination in part of the country between the Jordan River and the Mediterranean Sea. However, their right does not supersede the Jews' right, just as the Jews' right in the country does not supersede that of the Arabs.

Haaretz
June 13, 2017

Zionism was a rebellion against Jewish passivity. To the Jewish people, Zionism carried the message that they need not wait for the Messiah. Rather, they should be their own Messiahs. Zionism, born of the enlightenment, embodied the idea of human agency. Rather than wait for God or Messiah to bring about their salvation, Zionism called upon the Jewish people to be the vehicles of their own redemption. Zionism demonstrated that, even when dealt some of the worst cards in history, humans were active agents, capable of changing the course of their private and collective futures.

The Tower
December 15, 2016

The idea of Jews as active players in history — as masters of their fate — still grates on the consciousness of peoples and civilizations that were structured on the presumption that the Jews should have headed to the dustbin of history. For too many, the story that Jews could attain something for themselves by operating, as all peoples do, on multiple fronts — diplomatically, economically, militarily — is still so fanciful that to some, the story of Israel only makes sense if presented as a series of handouts by foreign powers with shady motivations. To the chagrin of those who want to put the Jews back "in their proper place," the State of Israel came into being precisely because Zionist Jews were done entrusting their fate to others.

The Algemeiner
November 2, 2017

No, Maestro, the Holocaust Did Not Create Israel

Daniel Barenboim is a Zionism denier. Zionism denial is the claim he raised in his opinion piece ("Germany is repaying its post-Holocaust debts to Israel – but not to the Palestinians," June 8) saying that Israel exists because of the Holocaust.

Zionism denial is the story of how the State of Israel "was given" to the Jewish people by the guilt-ridden world after the Holocaust. Zionism denial is also the claim that the Palestinians are also the victims of Germany and Europe, for without the Holocaust, their catastrophe would have been avoided.

The upshot of Zionism denial is ignoring the history of the Zionist movement before World War II. The denier completely ignores the fact that save for the decisive aspect of independence, the State of Israel in the making would have existed in fact on the eve of World War II. Zionism denial means ignoring that the State of Israel arose on the force of the vision, desire and uncommon deeds of far-sighted Jews, who laid the foundations of its independence.

Israel was not "given" to the Jews, because, among other things, the last thing on the agenda of the European nations at the end of the world war was guilty feelings toward the Jews. In certain European countries, these feelings began to crop up after a generation, and there have been no reports of guilty feelings in other countries until today. Just as India and Pakistan and other nations did not need the murder of a third of their people to receive a country at that time, the Jewish people would have obtained its own state at the end of World War II, not because of the Holocaust but rather because of another result of the war, the dismantling of the British empire.

> *Zionism denial robs the Jewish people of the recognition that Jews can, by force of vision, desire and work return to history as an active agent and shape a future in which they are not the victims of others.*

Zionism denial is not only ignoring the pre-war history of Zionism but also a theft of the Zionist consciousness from the Jewish people – the recognition that Jews can, by force of vision, desire and work return to history as an active agent and shape a future in which they are not the victims of others. Zionism denial means that the State of Israel becomes a "gift" that was given to the Jews because of what was done to the Jews by others – not for what the Jews did by and for themselves.

Worse than that, Zionism denial seeks to return the Jews to their "rightful" place in European history, as tolerated people whose fate is set by those who give and take as they please. Zionism denial turns Israel – alone among all countries in the world – into a conditional state, which is permitted to exist as long as those who received it, by grace and not by right, find favor in the eyes who "gave" them the country.

Zionism denial also robs the Arabs, and the Palestinians amongst them, of their status as people of an ancient and independent culture, whose positions and actions have consequences. From the Arabs' perspective, the meaning of accepting the principle of partition was to rise above centuries of cultural construction by which the Jews were followers of an inferior religion, which was permitted to exist by the grace of the majority, and by a long-established custom in which it was only possible to live with the Jews as long as they knew their place as people who are not and cannot be equal to Muslims and Arabs.

It is true that given that there were more Arabs than Jews in the Land of Israel, the Arabs did not have an incentive to compromise and to split this land with the Zionist movement. But the fact that from this perspective they had reasons to reject the partition plan does not absolve them of responsibility for the outcome. Had they succeeded in rising above their history and not relying on their numerical superiority, they could have accepted the partition plan and not objected to it with force. The establishment of Israel would not have become their disaster.

There is a claim by which the partition map, in which there was a significant Arab minority within the

Jewish state, proves that the Zionist leadership planned on "cleansing" the territory of Arabs regardless of their assent to partition. This claim ignores the fact that at the same time hundreds of thousands of Jews sat in Displaced Persons camps in Europe and Cyprus, awaiting the establishment of the Jewish state and the opening of the gates of immigration. There was no need for cleansing, based on the partition map. What was needed was opening the door to Jews – a door that if not for the Arab struggle against Zionism before World War II, would not have closed in the first place.

The right of the Jewish people to have a country in its own homeland is a universal right, which is reserved for every people – the right to stand on its own authority and to control its fate. As long as the world is divided into some 200 countries, on the basis of the principle of self-determination for peoples and nations, the Jewish people have a right to this. The Palestinian Arabs also have a right to self-determination in part of the country between the Jordan River and the Mediterranean Sea. However, their right does not supersede the Jews' right, just as the Jews' right in the country does not supersede that of the Arabs.

When the Arabs recognize that the Jewish people have an equal right to self-determination in part of its homeland in the Land of Israel, they will certainly understand that they have to give up their demand for return to all parts of the State of Israel. Then they will be able to establish their country in part of Palestine, and legislate the Palestinian right of return just as the Jews did, thanks to their vision, labor and determination.

Haaretz
June 13, 2017

Jewish Action – Not Balfour – Created Israel

The campaign waged by Palestinians and their supporters to demand that Britain apologize for the Balfour Declaration, a century after it was issued, betrays yet again their fundamental misunderstanding of how and why the modern State of Israel came into being. Israel is the outcome of deliberate Jewish action — not of foreign hand-outs. Israel is a country attained — not a land given.

The Balfour Declaration — that short letter written in the fog of the Great War by Lord Balfour to Lord Rothschild, expressing His Majesty's Government's favorable view of the establishment of a Jewish homeland in the ancestral land of the Jews — demonstrates the remarkable manner in which Zionism was able, in a few short decades, to infuse Jews with a sovereign spirit.

Multiple explanations are given as to why, in 1917, the British foreign minister would write such a letter to a prominent Jew: anything from British antisemitism, to

British religious philo-Semitism, to British war interests. But all of these factors would have been irrelevant in the absence of deliberate Jewish Zionist action.

Without the preceding two decades of Zionist activism in making the case for Jewish self-determination in the Land of Israel, and without the Zionist can-do spirit of Chaim Weizmann, who deployed his connections and his powers of persuasion to that end, there would still have been British antisemitism, British religious philo-Semitism and British war interests, but no letter.

Moreover, without collective Jewish mobilization in the name of self-determination and liberation, that letter — along with many other promises, letters and declarations that were made by powerful nations toward less powerful peoples at the end of World War I — would have come to naught.

Nothing in what came next — the establishment of embryonic self-rule for Jews in the land; the League of Nations Mandate for Palestine; the immigration of Jews to the land; the building of cities, towns and agricultural collectives, as well as economic, political and cultural institutions; the establishment of a state in all but name; and independence on the eve of World War II; the United Nations' grudging support after the war for the establishment of a Jewish state in part of the land; and ultimately the establishment of an independent state of Israel in part of the land — was pre-ordained.

> *Israel is the outcome of deliberate Jewish action — not of foreign hand-outs. Israel is a country attained — not a land*

Faced with mounting diplomatic and violent

opposition, with a Britain that reneged on its commitments as soon it actually got its hands on the land, with forces that were determined to prevent the Jews from attaining liberty — each fragile achievement depended on the deep and abiding commitment of the Zionist Jews to their cause of national liberation, their collective mobilization to realize it, their deployment to that end of all manners of diplomatic, narrative, economic and military skills, and ultimately, their ability to remain focused on the singular goal of sovereignty and independence, even at the price of forgoing parts of the land to which they had a deep historical attachment and an internationally sanctioned claim.

The idea of Jews as active players in history — as masters of their fate — still grates on the consciousness of peoples and civilizations that were structured on the presumption that the Jews should have headed to the dustbin of history. For too many, the story that Jews could attain something for themselves by operating, as all peoples do, on multiple fronts — diplomatically, economically, militarily — is still so fanciful that to some, the story of Israel only makes sense if presented as a series of handouts by foreign powers with shady motivations.

To the chagrin of those who want to put the Jews back "in their proper place," the State of Israel came into being 31 years after the Balfour Declaration, precisely because Zionist Jews were done entrusting their fate to others. Through their actions, from 1917 on, the Zionist Jews simply said to Britain, and the world: "Thank you very much Lord Balfour. We'll take it from here."

The Algemeiner
November 2, 2017

Anti-Feminism and Anti-Zionism

Feminism and Zionism are cut from the same cloth. Both movements emerged from the same intellectual and political origins, they both exhibited similar growth trajectories, becoming two of the most successful revolutions to sweep and survive through the 20th century, both continue to face ferocious backlash, and both remain vibrant and necessary in the 21st century.

Feminism and Zionism are daughters of the enlightenment. They were born of that intellectual revolution against the inevitability of the human condition as one subject to a hierarchical, divinely ordained order, underpinned by a religious system and elaborate theology. Feminism and Zionism are rebellions against that order. They are both part of the modern overthrowing of a pre-modern order in which each living creature, born into a station and role in the superstructure of society, remains in that role, carries it out dutifully and does not challenge it. Feminism and Zionism are infused with resistance against the pre-Enlightenment idea that how you are born should determine how you die.

Feminism and Zionism are ongoing rebellions against millennia-long power structures that assigned women and Jews a "proper place" in society. For women, it was an order dating back to the beginnings of the agricultural era, that simultaneously enabled and necessitated their control as child bearing properties. For Jews, it was a theological, and by extension social, assignation of their inferior role by the two civilizations that emerged from Judaic monotheism, but also claimed to supersede it: Christianity and Islam. Having made the claim to be the bearer of a new truth, in the form of a new testament or a new uncorrupted prophecy, the two civilizations could not but develop an adverse attitude toward those Jews who refused conversion and rejected the claims of both these civilizations to be the better and truer interpretations of the original scriptures. Naturally, Christianity—the more direct descendant of Judaism—was more ferocious in its theological and social loathing to those remaining Jews who still would not accept Christ. But Islam too was clear in its theology, as well as legal, social, and symbolic structures, that Jews, even when tolerated, were certainly not, and could not be, the equals of Muslims.

Entire cultural structures—civilizations—were built on the edifice of female and Jewish inferiority—so

> *By changing the very image of what it means to be a woman or what it means to be a Jew, feminism and Zionism forced change on societies and civilizations that were predicated on a very specific and limited image of what it meant to be either of those things.*

much so, that these themes in their multitude of expressions were transparent to those who were raised into those structures. Themes that emphasized female submission and exalted the limited role assigned to women were reinforced in a myriad of ways from the most minute social norms, to legal structures, to almost every form of cultural output from poetry to painting to children's stories. It was this near endless replication of only one possible model of female human life that created a sense of inevitability. If one is born a woman destined to do one thing—bear children to her master, then one inevitably lives her life and dies a woman, having done only this one thing (if she is lucky), and it is by this thing alone that her entire value is judged.

Themes that emphasized the moral failure of the Jew were the staple of Christian and some Muslim cultural creations—from Scriptures to paintings to children's tales to linguistic idioms. Since the continued existence of the Jews implied a rejection of Christianity and Islam, the Jew could not be conceived of as a moral being choosing wisely between good and evil. At best, Jews could be tolerated as relics, headed for the dustbin of history, against the inevitable progress of Christianity and Islam. At worst, their continued existence was an intolerable offense, necessitating the exaction of a price. Most commonly, their inferior status, vulnerability, and persecution served as evidence to the fate that awaits those who persist in their rejection of the true path.

Feminism and Zionism challenged all that. They were both forms of refusal to accept the role that others have assigned to women and Jews. They were forms of self-assertion that cried out: I refuse to be seen how you wish to see me, I refuse to be that which you want me to be, I am not your inferior, I can be so much more than I am allowed to be, and I insist on being free to explore and make the most of my humanity.

In that, feminism and Zionism were built on self-definition and human agency. Both these movements could emerge only once the secular and radical idea that human beings, individually and collectively, are masters of their fate, was introduced. Once human beings could be conceived of as active agents of historical change, rather than passive receivers of divine fate, women and Jews could begin to formulate the notion that even if one might be dealt some of the worst cards in history, and by a whole lot of dealers, it does not mean that there is nothing to be done.

Entire cultures and civilizations were mobilized to drive a wedge between the "Good Woman" and the "Bad Feminist," between the "Good Jew" and the "Bad Zionist."

Something could be done, but for feminism and Zionism to challenge power structures that have existed for millennia and been predicated on women and Jews "knowing their place," they could only do so on the footsteps of the modern political revolutions embodying the ideals of liberty, equality, and group solidarity. True, neither women nor Jews were to be included initially in the ideals of equality, but once the ideal of the liberty of human beings from submission, the essential equality of human life, and the necessity of group solidarity and mobilization for achieving these goals, were introduced, it was impossible to prevent these ideas from being adopted even by those whom the revolution did not initially expect to include.

Feminism and Zionism arose from anger at this kind of hypocrisy. Feminism and Zionism developed as those claiming to espouse the ideals of equality and liberty and solidarity twisted themselves into ideological and religious knots to justify keeping women and Jews out of this new world. Feminism and Zionism came into their own as the logical trajectory of equality among human beings could not but be extended to those who could also lay legitimate claim to being human beings, even if somewhat different from the mold.

It was the growing ability of women and Jews to lay claim to being human beings worthy of equality and liberty, as well as their ability to mobilize their respective groups to make that claim, that made the success of their revolutions possible. As women became more literate and educated, with direct access to knowledge, it became harder to justify their exclusion from that which was considered worthy only of the literate—such as the right to vote or to attain higher education. Once women had the right to vote and they became highly educated it became harder and harder to exclude them from other areas of life.

For Jews, as the promise of integration and emancipation into European society led them to greater achievements from science to art to literature, their continued exclusion under the guise of the new "scientific" ideology of anti-Semitism, rather than plain old Christian or Islamic theology, became ever less tolerable. As Theodor Herzl and other Jews, who initially believed that they were lucky enough to live in an age of progress, equality, and tolerance, when they would no longer be excluded from full participation in the dominant society by virtue of being Jews, came to realize that while Europe spoke of equality, it failed to practice it, they realized that their true emancipation and liberation from dependency on others, would only be possible when they are truly masters of their fate, collectively governing themselves in a state of their own.

Alas, feminist women and Zionist Jews proved themselves ingrates. The more they attained, the more they wanted. Unable to celebrate what they were given, they exhibited an annoying tendency to not just care about being somewhat better off than before but to actually want true equality. It was a tendency that was often resisted by women and Jews themselves, who feared that the fragile achievements they already had would be endangered by movements that insisted on pressing ever forward. The "problem" with feminism and Zionism was that no matter how successful they were, what achievements they brought about for women and Jews, it never seemed to be enough.

This was especially exasperating to some, given that feminism and Zionism were two of the most successful revolutions to emerge from enlightenment thinking. What began as insane ideas of a mad few, became, over a breathtakingly short time, more broadly accepted. The achievements of both movements in each turn were remarkable, and of a nature that only a short while earlier would have been considered unthinkable and impossible. Wherever and whenever feminism and Zionism swept through societies, they turned them upside down and inside out. By changing the very image of what it means to be a woman or what it means to be a Jew, it forced change on societies and civilizations that were predicated on a very specific and limited image of what it meant to be either of those things.

That change was not always welcome. In fact, it was resisted at every turn, often violently, even ferociously. The more power—of various kinds—was amassed by women and Jews, the more their rise felt like an offense to the "proper order of things." The challenge of feminism and Zionism to millennia-long power structures was never going to go over unchallenged. It is in the very nature of power that no-one, ever, gives it up willingly and easily. If women and Jews seemed unable to know "their proper place" and intent on demanding more, then they must be placed back in "their proper place," and if needed, by force.

Feminism and Zionism started out as revolutions for changing the fate of women and Jews, but as they grew in power and faced growing backlash, they became revolutions for civilizational transformation.

It is, therefore, no coincidence that wherever and whenever women and Jews grew in prominence, their rise was met with increasing violence. The so-called Icelandic paradox of a country where women have the most rights and face the greatest incidents of domestic violence is no paradox at all. The fact that the greatest forms of violence against Jews came against the backdrop of their growing success and prominence is no accident either. Even in the lands of Islam, where Jews historically were better treated than in Christian lands (not a particularly high bar...), "trouble [to the Jews] arose when Jews were seen to be getting too much power," writes Bernard Lewis in *The Jews of Islam*. Lewis explains that "when a persecution occurred ... the usual argument was that the Jews had violated the pact by overstepping their proper place."

Therefore, it is no accident, he argues that "it is during the 19th and 20th centuries, when the *dhimmis* [protected Jews] were no longer prepared to accept or respect the rules, that the most violent and bloody clashes have occurred."

Direct violence has not been the only method by which the backlash against the aspirations of women and Jews to equality has been implemented. Various insidious ways, mostly transparent to those who grew up under cultural expressions designed to signal the proper place for women and Jews, were employed. From "The Beauty Myth" to religious "modesty" to sinister anti-Zionist intellectual assaults, entire cultures and civilizations were mobilized to drive a wedge between the "Good Woman" and the "Bad Feminist," between the "Good Jew" and the "Bad Zionist."

The difference between the Good and the Bad? Power. A "Good Woman" does not aspire to power; in fact, she feels uncomfortable with it and would be more than happy to forgo it. A "Good Jew" feels queasy with manifestations of Jewish power, and in the face of raw expressions of it rushes to declare his or her renunciation of Zionism. It is no accident that the forms of female and Jewish expressions that are most mocked, criticized, and denigrated are those that involve the expression of power. If the revolutions of feminism and Zionism are ever to be stalled, and even rolled back, women and Jews must come to feel uneasy with power.

It might be baffling to a 21st-century reader why movements that sought nothing more than equality should continue to face such ferocious backlash. Equality has come to sound so benign, obvious, a taken-for-granted marker of modern society. But when one understands that true equality leads inexorably to a redistribution of power and resources, then it becomes quite understandable why to "those accustomed to privilege, equality feels a whole lot like discrimination." To those young enough to never have known a world where and when equality was not the norm, it is even more difficult to appreciate the hangover effect of historical power structures. Young men in the West might no longer individually think that women are their inferiors, but they would need to exhibit remarkable blindness to argue that they do not inhabit a world in which the social structures, norms, and cultural output were shaped by this assumption. Young people who have only always known a powerful state of Israel might fail to comprehend how the obsession of large parts of Western and Islamic civilization with Israel is an expression of their inability, still, to come to terms with Jewish power, and are therefore prone to confusing cause and effect—thinking that the Western and Islamic obsession with Israel is about what Israel does, rather than about what Israel is: an expression of Jewish self-mastery and power.

It is in the nature of feminism and Zionism that they cannot rest until they have reached true equality: until the resources of power are redistributed so that women and Jews are no longer ever in danger of being put "back in their place." This can only be achieved with the transformation of the civilizational systems that have determined what that "proper place" is. This is why feminism does not stop with education, voting, reproductive rights, equal pay at work, and safety at work. The more it gains, the more it exposes how entrenched the assumption of female inferiority is in the structures of society, and the more it presses onward do dismantle them. This is why Zionism has not ended with the establishment of a state for the Jewish people, because the idea of equal sovereign Jews, governing a share of the Earth's land on their own, continues to be ferociously resisted by the large swaths of the two civilizations that were built on the assumption of Jewish disappearance, often with the declared intention of rolling back that Jewish "transgression" in the form of the State of Israel.

Feminism and Zionism started out as revolutions for changing the fate of women and Jews, but as they grew in power and faced growing backlash, they became revolutions for civilizational transformation. Neither feminism nor Zionism will or could rest until new civilizations—entire cultural systems—emerge to replace those that were predicated on the assumption of female and Jewish otherness and inferiority. Not until almost all men feel completely at ease with the idea of powerful women, and most Westerners and Muslims feel at ease with the idea of powerful Jews could these revolutions call it a day, and neither should they.

Tablet
January 9, 2018

Intersectional Power of Zionism

Zionism has a story to tell that is not only about Jews or for Jews. Zionism has a story to tell that, when properly understood, has the power to inspire people and peoples to great acts of daring and sacrifice. Zionism tells a simple story: Victimhood is not destiny. A history of marginalization, humiliation, discrimination, persecution, massacres, and even genocide can be transcended. A people, no matter how downtrodden, can find within themselves the power to change their future.

When the story of Zionism is told, continuity is often highlighted: the continuous presence of Jews in the Land of Israel, the ongoing yearning of a people in exile to return to their homeland, the unrelenting hope for the ingathering of a people from all corners of the earth to find redemption in an ancient land.

But Zionism is as much a revolution in Jewish life as a continuation of it. In the immediate aftermath of the Roman exile, the Judeans might have conceived of their return to Judea as a forthcoming possibility. But by the 19th century, the idea of return was sublimated into a

Messianic wish, expressed in ritual and prayer. One day, a descendant of King David would arise and lead the Jewish people out of a fragile existence into a life of dignified sovereignty in a land of their own. It was a passive hope that mandated no action.

Zionism was a rebellion against this Jewish passivity. To the Jewish people, Zionism carried the message that they need not wait for the Messiah. Rather, they should be their own Messiahs. Zionism, born of the enlightenment, embodied the idea of human agency. Rather than wait for God or Messiah to bring about their salvation, Zionism called upon the Jewish people to be the vehicles of their own redemption. Zionism demonstrated that, even when dealt some of the worst cards in history, humans were active agents, capable of changing the course of their private and collective futures.

And change their destinies they did. In a few short years, the Zionist movement put in place the foundations for the future state of Israel, from a fledgling parliament to a banking system. On the eve of World War II, the modern state of Israel existed in all but name and independence. Throughout this time, Jews from around the world immigrated—ascended—to the Land of Israel,

Precisely because of its potential intersectional power to inspire downtrodden people to take action for their own equality and liberty, Zionism has been subject to decades of persistent attacks.

launching a process that would ultimately lead the state to be home to nearly half of the Jewish people.

The inspirational power of Zionism lay not only in its call to action, but in its vocabulary of human equality, liberty, and dignity. Zionism called upon the Jewish people to take action to achieve their rightful place among the nations as equals—nothing more, nothing less. This was a simple, but compelling, argument: In a world where nations and peoples were increasingly considered to possess a universal right to sovereignty in states of their own, where they could enjoy liberty and dignity, free from the oppressions of empire, the Jewish nation possessed that right as well.

Precisely because of its potential intersectional power to inspire downtrodden people to take action for their own equality and liberty, Zionism has been subject to decades of persistent attacks. It is in the nature of power that no one ever gives it up willingly. When those who were previously deemed inferior challenge existing power relations, especially long-established ones, they will always face backlash, typically ferocious and violent. This is intended to dissuade them from internalizing the dangerous idea of equality, sending them back to their "rightful" place.

Because Zionism meant that the Jews had the gall to challenge civilizational structures that assigned them an inferior status, it too faced backlash, and had to deal with both physically violent and intellectually sinister manifestations. The backlash was designed not only to put the Jews back where they belong, but also to prevent the spread of its contagious ideas. If Zionism stands as proof of the human will to dignity, then its name must be besmirched and the reality to which it gave birth erased, lest others follow suit.

It is no accident that so many Jews, inspired by the revolutionary idea of Zionism, seek to share it with others, and bring forth its message that victimhood is not destiny. But when they find that they are refused entry to the room where those supporting causes of human equality and liberty gather, on account of their Zionism or support of Israel, their exclusion sadly bears witness to the success of the backlash. Those who exclude pro-Israel or Zionist Jews from supporting intersectional causes of downtrodden people are depriving themselves of the most powerful sources of inspiration to human action.

But Zionism is about rejecting a destiny of victimhood. The backlash against it, in all it ugly forms, should not deter those who understand its story from sharing its powerful message with all.

The Tower
December 15, 2016

Ahead of the Curve: Israel's Nationalism Is a Model to Emulate

Israel has one glaring problem: lousy timing. Most of Israel's apparent problems, certainly the ones its critics claim it has, emerge from Israel's repeated inability to be synchronized with prevailing global moods. But patience has its rewards—over time, as challenges facing Israel turn out to be global rather than local, Israel's failings appear so much less so, if at all.

Consider, as an appetizer, the minor but remarkably annoying issue of airport security. During the 1990s, when I was working on projects in Israel for a global consulting firm, senior partners of the firm would arrive in Israel for a two- to three-day stay to oversee the projects. They would invariably arrive angry. Fuming, really. "What is this crazy security you have at your airports? How dare they look in my bag? How do you ever expect to be part of the global economy if you carry on this way?" The Israelis among us would bow our heads in shame, apologize profusely and mumble something about necessity and terrorism.

Cut to 9/11. Cut to the shoe-bomber. Cut to the liquid terrorism plots. Having spent, since 2011, cumulative hundreds of hours waiting in airport security lines around the world, I can safely argue that that Israel's Ben-Gurion Airport is one of the world's sanest. No need to take off shoes or belts. No fussing with tiny liquid bottles. Ben-Gurion has a security system that has been honed through decades of battling terrorism, yet designed to enable the existence of an open society.

Indeed, consider the battle against terrorism more broadly: For much of its existence, Israel had to face not only terrorism, but also persistent criticism that it is too heavy-handed in its dealings with terrorism, too prone to "disproportional" response. The Patriot Act and the wars in Iraq and Afghanistan should have been sufficient to put that criticism to bed, but for me, it took having a close-up experience of terrorism abroad to better appreciate Israel's

Most of Israel's apparent problems, certainly the ones its critics claim it has, emerge from Israel's repeated inability to be synchronized with prevailing global moods. But patience has its rewards—over time, as challenges facing Israel turn out to be global rather than local, Israel's failings appear so much less so, if at all.

response. Several months ago, while on an extended stay in France, I was several feet away from the largest terrorist attack ever perpetrated by a single attacker, the Bastille Day massacre in Nice. A nineteen-ton white truck rampaged through a crowd of tens of thousands, killing families for two kilometers while meeting no resistance. As people were already lying dead, families throughout the Nice Promenade were enjoying the festivities, given no warning and having no sense of the impending danger.

In response, France declared an extended state of emergency, sent its army and various security forces to the street, mixing it with a bizarre campaign to hunt down women in burkinis on its beaches. Some officials even excused the gross incompetence that enabled the massacre by wondering, "How long could a country have its guard up?" To which one response was "The State of Israel, 68 years and counting." Indeed, witnessing the French response, I wanted nothing more than to return to Israel, and soon. I wanted to go back to a country where people knew that when a massive truck rams into a crowd, it is not a traffic accident—and the driver is shot on sight. I also wanted to live in a country that fights terrorism while enabling its Muslim minority to dress as they will.

Consider finally the question of nationalism. For years, if not decades, Israel has been subject to criticism for its supposed retrograde insistence on maintaining and fighting for a nation-state of the Jewish people. Jewish nationalism, also known as Zionism, was subject to a sustained onslaught as a singularly depraved idea. Even at its most benign, the criticism looked down on Zionism and Israel as a last vestige of a past world, where humans still cared for their nations and peoples, and were willing to sacrifice their very lives to sustain them. Quite a few critics conveyed the sense it was distasteful, bad manners really, on behalf of the pesky Jews to insist on their right to self-determination in a nation-state of their own. In a world committed to a post-national universalist vision, Israel supposedly stood out uniquely as an eyesore.

In fact, over the years, I have been asked by students of the world's top universities, why we in Israel were still insisting on this "passé" idea of a nation-state. My response was that as much as I share their desire to live one day in a John Lennon world with no religion and no countries and all the people living as one, I do get suspicious and somewhat antsy when the Jews are asked to go first.

It turns out that not only are the world's nations not embracing John Lennon's vision, but quite the opposite. Whether it's called populist nationalism, economic nationalism, or the return of the closed society, there is no doubt that this is the rising global tide. From Asia to the Middle East, Europe, and the United States, it is becoming increasingly clear that faced with globalization, immigration, and economic uncertainty, people have a greater need for a specific sense of belonging to something, whether it is a tribe, a people, or a nation. This basic need of all peoples can be expressed in a variety of forms, from the benign to the mean-spirited, but when it is ignored and even denigrated, it is more likely to manifest itself in supremacist and racist ways.

Taken against this backdrop, Israel's Jewish nationalism emerges as reasonably balanced: providing people with a sense of specific belonging to a people and a nation, while addressing ongoing challenges of immigration, integration, and the existence of large minorities who possess, at best, ambivalent attitudes towards Jewish nationalism. Decades of dealing with these enormous challenges under the world's magnifying glass while being subjected to scathing and often sinister criticism mean that if anything, Israel and the Jewish people are positioned to provide a model of a relatively benign form of nationalism. It is not that Israel does not exhibit distasteful expressions of nationalism; they are not cause for pride, but they can no longer be considered cause for specific shame. There is nothing in the Jewish need for a sense of tribal and national belonging that makes it inherently better or worse than that need among other peoples, tribes and nations in the world.

Ultimately, if there is anything particularly Israeli or Jewish about the state of Israel, it is that when global phenomena are addressed in Israel, it is with a bit of Jewish kvetch and Israeli improvisation. Those who criticize Israel as if there is something uniquely wrong with the Jews, Israel, and Zionism, simply miss the fact that our only real fault is lousy timing, and that it is all coming, sooner or later, to a theater near you.

The Tower
November 30, 2016

Shimon Peres and the Dreams That Live On

Shimon Peres symbolized possibility. He embodied the daring idea that the impossible could be made possible. It wasn't blind faith that led him on this path. It was experience. In his life he witnessed time and again how ideas and dreams, previously deemed insane, became taken-for-granted reality. Primarily among these was Zionism and the State of Israel. In the painful history of his family and in his early life, he experienced how the trodden-upon Jewish people found within themselves the audacity to dream big and act even bigger.

With his own two hands, he helped midwife a present for a Jewish people that was once a ridiculous future. He helped David Ben-Gurion win numerous political battles on the road to leading the Jewish people to freedom in their land. He made sure that the Jews fighting a war of annihilation, which the Arab countries waged against the nascent Jewish state, had the weapons they needed to ultimately prevail. He forged global alliances that made Israel more secure and had the gall to obtain for the beleaguered young state the ultimate weapon to secure its survival in a hostile region. But when decades later he recognized that the region might be turning somewhat less hostile, he grabbed the opportunity and brokered careful understandings between former sworn enemies.

Time and again he was ridiculed for his dreams. He couldn't care less. He was immune to ridicule. He knew that Theodor Herzl, who dreamt of a sovereign republic for the Jewish people, was ridiculed for his supposed delusions to his last day. Yet when everyone was wrong, Herzl was right. Shimon Peres was willing to bear ridicule, because he knew the future would prove him right. And even if not, he at least tried—and had fun doing so. Up to his last day, he retained a child's sense of wonder and fun. He enjoyed weaving grand visions and then going about realizing them. He enjoyed waking up every day (at 4:00 AM!) to a new day of action in the service of dreams.

Thanks to Shimon Peres's decades of work on behalf of Israel and its people, we are and will always continue to be a state and a people who make the impossible possible.

His dreams were not confined to security, defense, and peace. He loved arts, culture, and science. When I started working for him, his passion of the moment was nanotechnology. It was the manifestation at that time of his perennial infatuation with the future and all that is new and promising and full of possibility. He approached nanotechnology the way he approached all his grand ideas: with curiosity, relentlessness, and a plan for action. He did not let a single person who came to see him, whether it was a head of state or businessperson or poet, to leave the meeting without homework for advancing the cause of nanotechnology. Once, two people who came to Peres to discuss matters of the Jewish world, begged me to ask Shimon not to spend the entire meeting on nanotechnology. That did not happen, of course. But he was the one to get it, just as he did later when he took up the cause of neurology. His plans for action and relentlessness in achieving them made the difference.

Shimon Peres' greatest dream—to secure Israel's existence through a final-status peace agreement between it, the Palestinians, and the entire Arab world—remained outside his reach. He came tantalizingly close—or at least he believed he did—several times. The numerous setbacks, violence, wars, and loss of life did not deter him from actively seeking peace. Even when the majority of Israelis, including from his own political camp, reached the conclusion that the Palestinians are decades (if not centuries) away from giving up on their maximalist demands and still cannot stomach sharing the land with a sovereign Jewish people, he swept aside such conclusions as passive pessimism unworthy of Zionists. Many continued to admire his passion for peace, but wondered if all that energy was not being expended on a futile effort.

With the death of Shimon Peres, it is all too tempting to depict his death as sounding the death knell for the hope for peace. Some are already trying to promulgate this idea in their efforts to paint Israel as rejectionist. But peace did not die with Shimon Peres, just as it did not die when Yitzhak Rabin was assassinated either. The negotiation efforts of Ehud Barak and Ehud Olmert, and the advocacy of countless Israelis who support and fight for peace, have proven otherwise. Israel's yearning for peace—true peace—with its neighbors remains as powerful as ever.

As a founding father and active parent, Shimon Peres passed on his DNA to his country and his people. Some Israelis wonder whether his passing also means the passing of his spirit of possibility, but they need not worry. Thanks to Shimon Peres's decades of work on behalf of Israel and its people, we are and will always continue to be—in science, defense, culture, and peace—a state and a people who make the impossible possible.

The Tower

II. ON WHY THERE IS NO PEACE

A simple counting of 50 years of military occupation might lead reasonable people to believe that it can no longer be considered temporary. But that fails to take account of an alternative time frame: the Arab and Muslim countdown until the end of Zionism and the State of Israel. That countdown reflects the prevailing Muslim, Arab and Palestinian view that Zionism is a historical aberration that will not – and must not – last. Any Israeli effort to end the military occupation in a manner that would bring it peace and security thus clashes with the Muslim, Arab and Palestinian view that no place for compromise and agreement exists that would grant legitimacy to Zionism and the State of Israel and that would accept its permanence.

Fathom
Spring 2017

The Palestinian national movement remains committed to the idea of liberating all of Palestine, from the sea to the Jordan River. There is no sign that it and its leaders are prepared to recognize that the Jewish people, as a people, have an equal right to self-determination in this land, which is its birthplace too. The main indication of the Palestinian national movement's commitment to continuing the struggle for all of Palestine is its continued cultivation of the illusion of return — in particular, the perception that any Palestinian at all, including fourth-generation offspring of refugees living in Ramallah, will eternally have the non-negotiable, individual "right" to return to the motherland; to return anywhere in the land between the Jordan River and the sea. Holding onto the "right of return" enables the Palestinians to continue to believe that even if they lose a battle, the war isn't over. And if the war isn't over, there's no need to admit defeat, no need to sign an agreement of surrender.

Haaretz
September 22, 2016

Israel Will Stand Fast

A simple counting of 50 years of military occupation might lead reasonable people to believe that it can no longer be considered temporary. But that fails to take account of an alternative time frame: the Arab and Muslim countdown until the end of Zionism and the State of Israel. That countdown reflects the prevailing Muslim, Arab and Palestinian view that Zionism is a historical aberration that will not – and must not – last. Any Israeli effort to end the military occupation in a manner that would bring it peace and security thus clashes with the Muslim, Arab and Palestinian view that no place for compromise and agreement exists that would grant legitimacy to Zionism and the State of Israel and that would accept its permanence.

Time and the Muslim Arab 'No'

Zionism was always going to challenge human imagination. The story of an oppressed and persecuted people, living as guests among hostile host nations who found the will to rise-up, liberate themselves, and rebuild a sovereign nation in their ancient homeland, was bound to be viewed as either deeply inspiring or utterly insane. It is unsurprising that to the Muslims and Arabs who occupied the Land since their conquest of it in the seventh century, the story appeared insane. Not only were the Jews claiming to return home after two thousand years to a land in their midst, but the Jews represented a people whom the Muslim Arabs have, over centuries, come to view as their inferiors.

From the Muslim and Arab perspective, the Jews – who while not infidels deserving of death, had failed to accept the final prophecy of Mohammed – were naturally destined towards the dustbin of history. Until that happened, the Jews could live as a tolerated minority of lower status, under the protection of their Muslim superiors. Life could be relatively harmonious if Jews knew and accepted their lower status in the pecking order of the proper Muslim society.

The one thing that Jews were not supposed to do was challenge their place in society. To do so was to undermine the proper order of things and represented an affront to 'justice' as conceived in the Arab Muslim world. Initially, it was the imported colonial idea of emancipation that provided the Jews in Arab lands controlled by British and French with the dangerous idea that they were the equals of Arab Muslims. Later, it was Zionism. Either way, the response was violence, massacres, war, ethnic cleansing, and never-ending resistance. The idea of Jews as the equals of Muslim Arabs could not be allowed to stand.

Viewed in this context, the Muslim Arabs 'no' to an equal, sovereign, Jewish presence in their midst was to be expected.

From the Muslim Arab perspective, violent opposition towards challenges to the proper pecking order was both 'just' and numerically rational. Not only were the inferior Jews advancing an insane story of returning home after two thousand years, but in the first half of the 20th century they constituted only a few hundred thousand challenging an Arab nation of tens of millions, backed by a Muslim world numbering hundreds of millions. Viewed in this context, the Muslim Arabs 'no' to an equal, sovereign, Jewish presence in their midst was to be expected.

And 'no' it was. Throughout the first half of the 20th century the Arab world consistently rejected any plan that would lead to the establishment of a sovereign Jewish state in the sliver of land between the Jordan River and the Mediterranean Sea. It opposed the League of Nations Mandate and fought against Jewish immigration to the land at the most critical time in Jewish history, depriving tens – if not hundreds – of thousands of Jews of their only chance to escape from a Europe that was closing in around them. The only exception to this opposition came from the Hashemites, who viewed Zionism as a force for good in the wake of collapse of the Ottoman Empire, and as allies in building a new post-Ottoman order of sovereign peoples and states, but their position proved consistently too weak to openly break ranks with Arab rejectionism.

The violent Muslim Arab rejection of Jewish sovereignty in their midst reached a pinnacle with the war against partition. Initiated and waged by the Arabs, the war to prevent the nascent State of Israel coming into existence was the most organised and comprehensive attempt (at the time) by the Arab world to restore 'justice' and 'order' as they conceived it. Even after they subsequently lost the war, they refused to concede defeat and accept the Jewish state. A battle might have been lost, but the war had to go on.

In the negotiations following the war, the Arab negotiation teams not only refused to meet with representatives of the State of Israel, but took great pains to emphasise that the armistice lines separating the newly independent State from the Gaza Strip and the West Bank were not to be borders. Borders implied permanence. These were cease-fire lines only, because the war was not over. The message was clear: the Jewish people might have declared independence in the State of Israel, but sooner or later there would be another war that would erase that humiliating eyesore from the Arab region.

In the wake of the Arab defeat, the commitment to restore the proper Arab and Muslim 'order' meant a blanket Arab refusal to absorb the Arab refugees from the war, keeping them and generations of their descendants under the temporary status of 'refugees' for decades, so that one day they could 'return' and bring an end to Zionism. The concept that third and fourth generation Arabs, born in an Arab country, can be classed as temporary 'refugees' from another land was completely acceptable, since Israel itself was temporary, and an Arab Palestinian 'return' to the days when the State no longer existed was a tangible possibility. (Again, the only exception was Jordan, which was willing to absorb the refugees and end the war by establishing permanent borders, although King Abdullah was assassinated for his position, once again demonstrating to the Hashemites that they could not afford to break rank with Arab orthodoxy.)

This Arab rejectionist position also manifested itself in the vicious expulsion and ethnic cleansing of Jewish communities – almost all predating Islam and the Arab conquests of the region – from the Arab world. Jews – who were internalising the idea that they could win wars over Arabs and establish sovereign states where they had no masters – could no longer be trusted to stay in Arab lands and 'know their place'.

The establishment and growth of the State of Israel did little to undermine the idea that Jewish sovereignty, in what the Arabs and Muslims viewed as land that was exclusively their own, was a temporary aberration. Across the Arab and Muslim world Israel was subjected to economic and diplomatic boycotts and campaigns of terrorism designed to hasten its end. In Arab mythology, Israel was the second crusader state, and its fate was to be the same as its predecessor. It would last for a few short decades and then a new Salah-ad-Din saviour would restore the land to Islam and the Arabs would drive out the foreign crusaders from whence they came. All the Arabs had to do was to resist and be patient. Compromise and accept the permanence of Israel was not an option.

After 1967: The Arab Refusal to Say 'Yes'

The humiliating defeat of five Arab armies in 1967, and the loss of the Golan Heights, the West Bank, the Gaza Strip and the Sinai Peninsula in a short span of six days did nothing to change the basic Arab mythology of the temporary nature of Israel. While the western world was establishing the formula of 'land for peace', the Arab world clarified its rejection of it. What appeared to make sense to much of the West – that land acquired by Israel in the Six-Day War was a valuable asset that could be traded for the long-desired peace with the Arab world – made no sense to those who still considered the State of Israel temporary.

Even when the 'land for peace' formula was employed, as in the peace agreement with Egypt and Jordan, subsequent decades demonstrated that these were closer to 'we will no longer attack one another agreements,' rather than peace. The Arab world remained unable to treat the Jewish state as a genuine legitimate presence in its midst.

Most notably, on two separate occasions – in 2000 and 2008 – the Arab Palestinians refused to say 'yes' to Israeli proposals that would have ended the military occupation of the West Bank. These proposals demonstrated that the choice Israel made after the 1967 Six-Day War – to govern most of the territories of the West Bank and Gaza in the form of a military occupation (which is a legitimate form of governance of territories acquired in war which the victorious side does not intend to annex and keep) – reflected a perspective that these territories were assets to trade, rather than a homeland to annex. Although this view was not shared by all Israelis – especially the Messianic settler movement, for whom the acquisition of what they termed Judea and Samaria represented the completion of God's promise to his people – 'official Israel,' and the majority of Israelis, did not take actions to annex the territories (except around Jerusalem) and make Israel's presence there permanent. Moreover, with the 2005 disengagement from the Gaza Strip and northern West Bank, 'official Israel' demonstrated that even when it built settlements, these were reversible, especially if withdrawal from territories

It is necessary to demonstrate to the Muslim-Arab world that their view of history is wrong, and that rather than constituting a second crusader state, Israel is the sovereign state of an indigenous people who have come home.

would bring greater security to Israel within the pre-1967 lines.

For most Israelis, the repeated Palestinian failures to say 'yes' to clear and distinct opportunities to end the military occupation of the West Bank and Gaza, and to build a peaceful state for themselves in territories evacuated by Israel, reinforced the view that more than the Arab Palestinians wanted a state for themselves, they wanted to deny a state to the Jewish people. Seventy years after the British Foreign Secretary told Parliament on the eve of partition that 'for the Jews, the essential point of principle is the creation of a sovereign Jewish state', while 'for the Arabs, the essential point of principle is to resist to the last the establishment of Jewish sovereignty in any part of the land', it seems the Arab Palestinians still see no reason to compromise with a project they view as 'unjust' and temporary. After all, if the crusader state lasted 88 years (including Jerusalem), then in 2017 – when Israel will mark 69 years – all the Arab Palestinians have to do is wait a mere 19 more years until the second crusader state will disappear.

Given the Arab understanding of Zionism as a temporary historical aberration whose life span is a mere few decades, it made sense for the Palestinians to repeatedly choose to suffer the daily humiliations of living under a military occupation rather than to accept the far greater humiliation of permanent Jewish sovereignty on land they considered exclusively their own. In refusing to end the military occupation by making a permanent peace with Israel, the Arab Palestinians were making a conscious choice that was based on their understanding of Arab history and Islamic 'justice'. As Arabs and Muslims, the Palestinians were not hapless victims, but rather masters of a historical narrative, at the end of which their resistance and patience would be rewarded with victory, in the form of Zionism's disappearance. While they might suffer in the interim period, the choice they made was for what they perceived as the far greater good – defeating Zionism and driving away the sovereign Jewish presence from their land.

How to End the Occupation: Stand Fast, Stand Longer

How can a temporary 50-year military occupation of most of the West Bank by Israel come to an end, if the Muslim, Arab and Palestinian view of history is that 50 years of Israeli occupation matters significantly less than the countdown of the remaining 19 years on the crusader clock? It is necessary to demonstrate to the Muslim-Arab world that their view of history is wrong, and that rather than constituting a second crusader state, Israel is the sovereign state of an indigenous people who have come home. This can only be achieved through Jewish power and persistence over time. And given the vast numerical imbalance between Jews and Arabs, it can only be achieved if those who truly seek peace support the Jewish people in sending the message to the Arab world that the Jewish people are here to stay.

The essence of the conflict between Zionism and the Muslim Arab world is a battle over time, a race of mutual exhaustion. The question that will determine how the conflict is ultimately resolved revolves around who will give up first: will the Zionists give up on their project in the face of unrelenting violent resistance, or will the Muslim Arabs give up on their project of erasing the sovereign Jewish presence in their midst, and finally come to accept it as a part of their history, rather than an affront to it?

Only time will tell.

Fathom
Spring 2017

The War Isn't Over Yet

Anyone who wants to understand why the conflict between the Zionist movement and the Palestinian Arabs has been going on for over 100 years won't find the answer in learned discussions of the question as to whether a quarter, a third or half of the Arabs were expelled during the 1948 War of Independence.

Anyone who wants to understand how only as a result of that conflict there are millions of people today claiming to be refugees from a war that ended decades ago, while most of them are descendants who were never expelled, won't find the answer in a study that investigates whether the residents of some village or other were expelled or fled, how and when.

Even worse: Anyone who focuses on these details on the assumption that they can explain why the problem continues to this day, or tries to figure out why the Israeli-Palestinian conflict is unique, falls into the trap of those who deliberately tried to perpetuate the problem in the first place.

Throughout the 20th century, and especially beginning in mid-century, during the decline of empires, liberation of nations and birth of countries, forced population exchanges were an accepted means of drawing the new borders, and were even considered an essential stage in ensuring peace. Tens of millions of people were removed from their homes, sometimes with great cruelty, and forced to go into exile dozens and thousands of kilometers away, without getting another opportunity to go back and see what they had considered their homeland for hundreds of years.

That was the case in the huge transfer between India and Pakistan in 1947, during which no fewer than 15 million people became refugees. That was the case in post-World War II Europe: Over 12 million Germans were expelled from Eastern Europe and over a million Poles left Ukraine, Lithuania and Belarus. Hundreds of thousands of Chinese people fled from China after the Communists came to power in 1949, and over a million fled from North Vietnam to South Vietnam in the early 1950s.

None of these situations gave rise to a "refugee problem" that hasn't been solved to this day. None of the millions who became refugees in the 1940s are seriously asking to return to their previous homes, and certainly they don't receive international recognition and institutional support for such a demand. Slowly but surely, sometimes with the gnashing of teeth, the refugees were rehabilitated in the countries where they found refuge and began their lives again.

The unique nature of the Palestinian refugee problem and the reason for its continuation to this day are therefore unrelated to the circumstances of its creation: Even if Arabs were expelled during the war, that expulsion wasn't exceptional in the global context – not in its scope, and certainly not in its cruelty. On the contrary, the Palestinian Arabs themselves carried out total ethnic cleansing against the Jews, and did not leave a single Jew in the territory remaining in their hands at the end of the war in 1949.

That was also the fate of many Jews who had lived in Arab countries for hundreds and thousands of years: Many of them were expelled or had to leave due to the hostile attitude of the local population and the Arab governments, and found refuge in Israel.

The Palestinian refugee problem, and particularly its continuation, is a result of an Arab and Palestinian decision to convey a clear message: The war isn't over yet.

The problem of the Palestinian refugees, its centrality in Palestinian awareness and the fact that it is so acute can be understood only in their context within the Palestinian narrative. According to the Palestinians, this was not one of the usual, if regrettable, side-effects of wars, along with the dead and wounded; that's why it's different and cannot be compared to the death and expulsion of Jews in that very same war.

The expulsion and flight of the Palestinians is seen as part of a foreign imperialist plot, of which Zionism was the representative and in the first place was meant to expel a native people from its land. The Palestinians refuse to see their departure from the land as something that happens during wars (in their case, the side that started the war and lost was the side that left), but as part of a conspiracy by a population group that had no rights to the land, which forced itself on a country that didn't belong to it.

The departure of the Arabs from the country during the war, whether through expulsion or flight, has become a symbol of the injustice which, according to them, characterizes the entire Zionist project. The deliberate Arab decision to continue to be refugees and not to be rehabilitated during all the decades that have passed since the end of the war was and remains a clear political statement, which means nonrecognition of the outcome of the war that centered around the right of the Jewish people to self-definition, at least in part of its homeland.

The Palestinian refugee problem, and particularly its continuation, is not a result of the events of the war itself, but of an Arab and Palestinian decision to convey a clear message: The war they began 69 years ago this week in response to the United Nations Partition Plan, a war whose objective was to prevent the Jewish people from realizing its right of self-definition in its homeland – that war isn't over yet.

Co-Written with Adi Schwartz
Haaretz
December 2, 2016

The Israeli Left Wants the Palestinians' Defeat Too

The Zionist left wants to see the defeat of the Palestinian national movement just as badly as the right wing does. Only when it admits that, will the left be able to lead the State of Israel to a peace deal, if and when that becomes feasible. That is because a peace agreement based on dividing the land will be possible only when the Palestinian nationalist movement acknowledges its defeat to the Jewish nationalist movement – Zionism.

In general, the left prefers not to think or talk in terms of victory and defeat. The people on the left prefer to think that they are decent folk, people of compromise. The left views its support for dividing the land as a fair compromise, in

Unfortunately, what the left perceives as a fair compromise is perceived on the Palestinian side as a humiliating defeat.

which each party acknowledges that because of the other's existence, one side can't have it all.

Unfortunately, what the left perceives as a fair compromise is perceived on the Palestinian side as a humiliating defeat.

From the Palestinian perspective, the compromise suggested by the left is not essentially different from the right's dreams of empire. Both insist, for some reason, on the insane idea that the invented Jewish people have some unclear entitlement to self-determination in Arab Palestine, and it does not matter if it's over 17% of the area west of the Jordan River (the Peel plan), 55% (the partition plan), 78% (the 1967 boundaries) or 100%.

The Palestinian national movement remains committed to the idea of liberating all of Palestine, from the sea to the Jordan River. There is no sign that it and its leaders are prepared to recognize that the Jewish people, as a people, have an equal right to self-determination in this land, which is its birthplace too.

The main indication of the Palestinian national movement's commitment to continuing the struggle for all of Palestine is its continued cultivation of the illusion of return — in particular, the perception that any Palestinian at all, including fourth-generation offspring of refugees living in Ramallah, will eternally have the non-negotiable, individual "right" to return to the motherland; to return anywhere in the land between the Jordan River and the sea. Holding onto the "right of return" enables the Palestinians to continue to believe that even if they lose a battle, the war isn't over. And if the war isn't over, there's no need to admit defeat, no need to sign an agreement of surrender.

The right of return thus creates the broadest base of consensus on both sides: the Palestinians in supporting it, and the Zionists in opposing it. People on the left, like me, who are committed to dividing the land based on the 1967 borders, are also unwilling to accept the principle of the right of return.

It isn't only the Zionists: Non-Zionist left wingers who promote the vision of a single state, like Rogel Alpher for example, are not prepared to accept the right of return either, and urge the Palestinians to stop handing down a heritage of nakba from generation to generation, in exchange for abolishing the Israeli right of return.

Meanwhile, judging by the exchange of letters between Alpher and the Arab Israeli rapper Tamer Nafar, the non-Zionist left is prepared to forgo the right of return (for Jews) but expectations of Palestinian reciprocity in the form of forgoing their right of return, have been dashed.

The people of the Zionist left need to look in the mirror and admit this to themselves: We aren't nice; we aren't generous; we aren't fair. We, no less than the right, want the Palestinians to be defeated. We, no less than the right, demand they surrender and acknowledge that they aren't going to get the whole of Palestine. We insist on our right to self-determination in our homeland. Our right is not exclusive and is not supreme, but as long as the Palestinian nationalist movement denies it, we will seek its defeat. And then we will make peace.

Haaretz
September 22, 2016

One State Versus Two States

If Jews and Arabs are to exist peacefully and achieve justice in the framework of a single democratic state, as proposed by Perry Anderson, the acceptance by both peoples of the equality of the other, both as collectives and as individuals, is a necessary condition.

If Jews and Arabs are to draft a constitution that would be more than a useless piece of paper and which would secure their joint lives together, they must recognise each other as equal claimants to the land, and must recognise each other as people of equal value, regardless of their differences. Such an agreement is necessary because both peoples would be forfeiting their universal right to self-determination in a nation state of their own, for the purpose of living together in a single state. Both would need to have assurances beyond reasonable doubt that their rights as individuals and as a collective would be secured in a single state.

If either Jews or Arabs living in a territory under a single governing framework operate under the belief that the other people as individuals, are not their equals, and that as a collective they do not possess the equal right to be in the territory of the state, they would merely use the mechanisms of the state, as well as violence, to oppress the other people and try to push them out of that territory. Peaceful democratic life together would not be possible.

The intellectual argument for a one-state solution collapses if any of the sides can demonstrate they have good reason to believe that the single-state framework would deny them justice and equality. When religious supremacist Jews argue for a one-state solution, conveniently excluding Palestinians in Gaza and the Diaspora and offering convoluted responses to the questions of whether there will be civic equality for all, Arabs can make a very strong case that such a 'solution' is not promoted in good faith, and that Palestinian Arabs could not expect to be treated justly or equally in such a state.

That is more than enough to reject any such plans.

The reverse is equally true: when Arab Palestinians, or left-wing intellectuals who claim to uphold the Arab Palestinian cause, promote a one-state solution (even if only as a rallying cry), in which, as a result of immigration and growth rates, Arabs would quickly be the majority and Jews would live as a minority, the burden of proof lies squarely with the Arabs. Jews have every right to ask if they would be treated justly and equally in a single Arab majority state.

Can they make a compelling case that they can be entrusted with the equal treatment of Jews in a single state in which the Arabs are a majority? No.

To be fair, even today, very few countries in the world could make such a compelling case. (It is for precisely this reason that the Jews insist on realising their universal right to self determination.) Even those very few countries that could demonstrate their ability to treat Jews as equals and protect their rights, have only fully done so in recent decades, and among them even fewer countries appear substantially secure from the danger of reversal of their equal treatment of Jews. Indeed, the very few countries on this list are the only ones where Jews live and prosper in large numbers.

No Arab country is on that list. Jews, as individuals, have never been treated as the equals of Arabs in any country where Arabs have been a majority. Jews, as a collective, were never accepted as an equal people: equal to Arabs in their claim to their ancestral land or equal in their claim to any part of the decaying Ottoman Empire, where they both lived. Arab society has continuously denied the idea that the Jews are their equals as individuals, and have certainly and violently denied the notion that the Jews are a people and a nation, of equal standing to the great Arab nation or the various Arab nations.

A mythology reigns in some circles, promulgated at times by the Arabs themselves, that Jews and Muslims lived for centuries in harmony in Arab lands. The implication is that were it not for Zionism, this could have continued. It is akin to the myth promulgated by Margaret Mitchell of the harmony of blacks and whites in *Gone with the Wind*. To the extent any such harmony existed

Mutually accepted collective and individual equality is as much a necessary condition for the success of the two-state solution as it is for the one-state solution, if any is to be a solution at all.

between Jews and Muslims in the Arab world, it emerged from Jews acknowledging and accepting their subordinate status as inferior 'Dhimmis', tolerated and protected by

Muslims as 'people of the book' (rather than being killed or forcefully converted as infidels). As long as Jews accepted their status as 'protected subservient people' to the Arab Muslims, and it was clear who was the master and called the shots, they could live in relative harmony. It is a harmony that could only endure as long as those considered inferior did not have the gall to claim their equality.

The Arab Muslim world can definitely demonstrate extended periods in history when it treated the Jews better than had Christian Europeans, and could pride itself on not having committed industrial genocide of the Jews – albeit that is quite a low bar – but it cannot make any claim that it ever saw or treated the Jews as genuine equals.

The so-called harmony between subordinate and superior was indeed disturbed when the Jews, first under colonial rule, which introduced the idea of emancipation, and later with the rise of Zionism, dared to claim their equality. The preposterous Jewish claim to equality with Muslims in Arab lands led to the rise of violence, blood libels and pogroms against the Jews, culminating in the ethnic cleansing, property confiscation and expulsion of the Jews from Arab lands – approximately one million in number, some in communities which pre-dated Islam – in revenge for the greatest transgression of all: the Jewish insistence that they are a people and a nation, no less than Arabs. Moreover, that they have a right to a sovereign state of their own in a small corner of the disintegrating Ottoman Empire, which also happens to be their ancestral homeland, and which the Arabs have considered their own, since their conquest of it in the seventh century.

Ever since, Arab society has continually denied that the Jewish people are their equals as a people, accepting them as members of a religion only, and denying their collective rights in their land, arguing that the Jews are not a people of the land, but foreigners, with no connection to it. Zionism was not the source of Muslim Arab attitude towards Jews – it merely forced that attitude into sharp relief.

The 1947 UN partition, and all other subsequent offers and opportunities of partition between a Jewish state and an Arab state were denied, not on account of the inequitable division of the land, but on account that a Jewish state in any part of the land – whether it be on 1 per cent or 99 – was considered an insult. The Jewish claim of equality with the Arabs as a people has been the fountain of the persistent refusal of Arab and Palestinian leaders to accept any two-state solution, whether in 1947, 1967, 2000 or 2008.

The casual assumption that Arab Palestinian leaders have at any point truly accepted the two-state (as in a Jewish state and an Arab state) solution, and that Israel is at fault for killing off this option through settlement building – rehearsed here by Anderson – conveniently ignores the fact that the Arab Palestinians never accepted the two states for two peoples solution, nor any agreement that would create a Palestinian state – if such an agreement entails the final acceptance that the land would be shared with a Jewish state. At least in 1947 the Arab states had the integrity to publicly admit that their rejection of partition was based on the conviction that *any* Jewish state, of *any* size, was an intolerable insult.

But perhaps Jews should ignore all this baleful history and look with optimism to the present? Unfortunately, there is little in today's Arab world which inspires confidence that the Arabs are transcending their past and are willing to include and protect minorities. Anderson ignores the blunt truth: today, violence is engulfing the Arab world and is leading to the ethnic cleansing and genocide of minorities who are considered inferior to (Sunni) Muslim Arabs. Ancient Christian peoples and sects are being expelled and killed, and the only minorities capable of avoiding this fate are those which possess arms.

So if no-one can point to a moment in history when Jews were treated as equals by Arabs, whether individually or as a collective, and the present appears even worse than the past, on what grounds should we follow Anderson and urge the Jews to 'rely on the kindness of strangers', entrusting their fate to those who refuse to recognise them as a people with a legitimate claim to the land and well as their individual equals?

None.

The partisans of the so-called 'one-state solution' are blind to the necessary condition for two peoples living peacefully in one state: mutually accepted collective and individual equality. Since that necessary condition does not exist, the one state framework would merely serve to change the title of the conflict from the Israeli-Palestinian conflict to the Jewish-Arab civil war. It would solve nothing.

Ultimately, there are two peoples, tribes, and nations on this land. Whatever argument each side makes about the invented nature of the other, it is clear that at the very least, each side sees itself as distinct and different from the other people in that land. Both believe they have the legal, emotional, historical, and just claim to the entirety of the land. Save for a few rare and courageous individuals, the Palestinians believe that the Jews have no legitimate claim to the land. The Jews are generally divided on the issue of the legitimacy of the Arab claim. This says nothing about their respective moral nature – merely their differing regional realities. The Jews are keenly aware of their minority status in the region; they can ill afford to ignore the Arabs. The Palestinians, who live in a region where Arabs enjoy predominance, believe they can continue to imagine that the Jews are foreigners and crusaders who will not endure.

Justice and peace can only be served once both sides acknowledge the equal and legitimate claim of the other to the land, and their status as equals, both as collectives and as individuals. They will both have to accept that neither can have it all and that their right to all of the land is limited by the existence of another people with that equal right. This will happen one day, but not before each side has given up on the delusion that the other will somehow, someday be made to disappear.

Once both sides recognise the equal rights of the others as collectives and individuals to all of the land, and accept that neither can have it all, they can then figure out how best to organise their lives in a way that maximises their own hopes and dreams while leaving room for those of the other. After all, this is as much a necessary condition for the success of the two-state solution as it is for the one-state solution, if any is to be a solution at all. So whether the best way to organise the lives of Jews and Arabs in the land is by means of two states, one state, confederation, federation, economic union, or any other imagined idea, those are the details that can and should only be figured out by both sides. As much as the Jews need to be held to account on this issue of equality, it is time to demand that Arabs too demonstrate that they are willing to treat the

Jews as their equal claimants to the land and as their individual equals. More than the fate of the people of Israel and Palestine depends on it: the fate of the entire Arab world, its liberty and prosperity, depends on whether Arabs in general, and Sunni Muslim Arabs in particular, can accept in their midst those who are different from them, both as collectives and as individuals, and treat them as their equals.

Fathom
Spring 2016

Alongside or Instead of Israel: Which Palestine Is the U.N. in Solidarity With?

Only twice in history was the territory between the Jordan River and the Mediterranean officially called 'Palestine,' and neither was for an Arab or Muslim entity of any kind. The first related to the end of Jewish sovereignty over the land, and the second related to its prospective renewal.

The Roman Emperor Hadrian was the first to make official use of the name 'Palestine' or 'Palestina' to refer to the region between the Jordan River and the Mediterranean. To secure the end of Jewish resistance to the Roman Empire he not only quashed their revolt and forced them into exile, but he dismantled the Province of Judea, as it was called at the time, and renamed it Palestina. This name was taken from the writings of the Greek historian Herodotus, referring to the Biblical and Egyptian 'Pleshet' or land of the 'Philistines' on the southern coast (near present day Gaza). During the following centuries of

Arab and Ottoman domination of the region it was no longer called Palestine but the southern part of 'Al-Sham,' or greater Syria (the territory claimed now by the Islamic State).

The only other political entity in the Middle East to bear the name Palestine was the British Mandate, constituted in 1920 by the League of Nations, for the express purpose of effecting 'the establishment in Palestine of a national home for the Jewish people.' The Mandate allowed Britain the option of cutting the territory east of the River Jordan out of the mandate for a Jewish national home, which it duly exercised two years later, with the creation of Transjordan, today's Jordan. This step actually further serves to emphasize the connection between the name Palestine and the project of Jewish

> *These two versions of Palestine differ not just in their territorial ambitions, but in their essence. The first is a project of national liberation. The second is a project of national elimination.*

national liberation in the historic homeland of the Jewish people: land which was now closed to Jewish settlement no longer bore the name Palestine, and Palestine itself had – from that point in 1922 until the end of the mandate in 1948 – the borders that today encompass Israel, the West Bank, and the Gaza Stip. These borders are often referred to 'historic Palestine'. Usually without mentioning that they are 'historic' only insofar as they lasted for barely three decades, were governed by a European superpower, and delimited as the future national home for the Jewish people.

In the years of the mandate, both Jews and Arabs in Palestine were referred to as Palestinians. There was a mass-circulation Arab daily called *Falastin* and a popular Jewish one called *The Palestine Post*. Jewish organisations as diverse as the Philharmonic and the fledgling Football League had the word Palestine in their names too.

Neither a restoration of Roman Palestine nor of British Palestine, however, is the intention of the International Day of Solidarity. Instead, its intended focus lies in the ambiguity between two other versions of Palestine, both potential states and both expressions of the self-determination of the Arab Palestinian people.

The first version of Palestine is the state that could emerge in the West Bank and Gaza Strip, those parts of Mandatory Palestine conquered by Arab armies in 1948 and subsequently by Israel in 1967. Nearly the entire international community supports the establishment of such a state, ideally as the outcome of peace negotiations with Israel. The establishment of a Palestinian Authority in 1994 following the Oslo Accords laid down the political infrastructure of such a future state: it already has a government, a flag and its own stamps and passports; before its leadership rejected a final status agreement and embarked on a suicidal (in every sense of the term) terror campaign in 2000.

The second Palestine is the one which most Palestinian activists speak about, and, if realised, it would mean the end of Israel as the sovereign state of the Jewish people. It would be an Arab state on the entire territory between the Jordan River and the Mediterranean Sea, and come into being by superseding and erasing the present State of Israel. The borders of such a Palestine can be seen in the logos of all the leading Palestinian organisations –

'radical' and 'moderate' alike. This is the Palestine of the demonstrators who chant, 'From the River to the Sea, Palestine will be free.' It is the Palestine that activists imagine when they demand 'Justice for Palestine', a code phrase for bringing an end to Israel as the sovereign state of the Jewish people – the injustice that those Palestinians seek still to correct. It is the Palestine to which the Arab refugees from the 1947-1949 war and their millions of descendants today demand to 'return' so that the Jewish people would no longer have a sovereign nation in which they are a majority. The fate of any Jewish minority left in such a Palestine would be even worse than that of Jewish minorities in other Arab countries in the past century, if only because the persecuted Jews of Iraq and Yemen and North Africa had the State of Israel to flee to.

These two versions of Palestine differ not just in their territorial ambitions, but in their essence. The first is a project of national *liberation* which would confer upon a currently stateless people the self-determination it should have attained more than half a century ago by the necessary acceptance of a parallel project of national liberation next door. The second is a project of national *elimination*, directed against the same neighbouring project, under the genuine belief that the most important goal is not the attainment of a state for the Palestinian people but the denial of one for the Jewish people.

Which Palestine does the International Day of Solidarity promote? The text of the original 1977 resolution, drafted in the era of automatic Soviet and Arab-backed majorities in the UN General Assembly and with references to the 'inalienable rights of the Palestinian people including the right of return' leaves little doubt as to the original intention. And the rhetoric of today's activists is, if anything, even more menacing.

At the same time, the date chosen for the International Day of Solidarity, whatever the original intentions might have been, opens an option for a more constructive kind of solidarity. On 29 November 1947, the UN General Assembly voted to end the British Mandate over Palestine and replace it with two sovereign nation-states, one Arab and one Jewish – neither had a name yet. The Jews accepted this plan and endeavoured to build their state, which declared independence on the last day of the Mandate nearly six months later. The Arabs rejected partition and embarked on a war of extermination against the Jewish population of Palestine – and lost.

Perhaps, on this Day of Solidarity we can acknowledge the fact that this choice; not just the rejection of the specific partition plan of 29 November 1947, but the obsessive and violent rejection of Israel in any form, has been a terrible mistake. The world faces a choice: solidarity with *liberation Palestine* or with *elimination Palestine*. It must choose the former.

Co-Written with Shany Mor
Fathom
Autumn 2014

III. ON WHAT ISRAEL SHOULD DO

The survival of Zionism has always depended on waging and winning wars on no less than two fronts. Today, Israel's survival depends on Jews and lovers of Israel doing the same: fighting Jewish maximalists at home and fighting Arab maximalists abroad with the same passion and vehemence. This should be the new standard for those who oppose both forms of maximalism. Jewish organizations that claim to promote a two-state solution should demonstrate that as much as they are fighting settlements, they are also fighting Arab maximalism. Jewish organizations that defend Israel and fight Arab maximalism shouldn't be afraid to take a stand against Jewish maximalists, if they wish to do so. Those among us who believe that a Jewish people that wants it all risks being left with nothing shouldn't have to choose their battles. We can save Zionism by defeating Jewish maximalists at home and Arab maximalists the world over.

The Tower
February 22, 2017

We need a clear map showing Israel's eastern border and the limits of its territorial demands. West of the border will include annexed land where full citizenship is granted. To the east we need a policy of "yes to the occupation, no to the settlements." This policy recognizes the existence of another people between the Jordan River and the Mediterranean Sea but also recognizes that a long time will pass until this people agrees to the division of the land with the Jewish people. This policy understands that land must be left for the other side, but Israel must remain militarily in the territory until its adversaries lay down their arms. This is a return to Zionism's basic principles; people who take responsibility for their fate without waiting for the Messiah or God to solve their problems.

Haaretz
December 31, 2016

How to Fight Jewish Maximalists at Home and Arab Maximalists Abroad

One state? Two states? What's a Jew to do? What should a Jew in Israel or abroad do? What should any lover of Israel do? What should anyone who cares deeply about the remarkable achievement of renewed Jewish sovereignty in the Land of Israel and wants to protect it from those who would destroy it do? The answer to the perplexed is to fight Jewish maximalists at home and Arab maximalists abroad.

The future of the State of Israel is under attack from within and without. From within, Israel faces the danger of too much love. There are those who supposedly love the Land of Israel so much that they need to own all of it. These are the Jewish maximalists. It is not security that concerns them or the question of defensible borders. Instead, they are imbued with a messianic zeal that compels them to settle and eventually annex the territories between the Jordan River and the Mediterranean Sea over which Israel is not sovereign: Judea and Samaria to them, the West Bank to the rest of the world.

For Jewish maximalists, Zionism is less about Jewish sovereignty *in* the Land of Israel than Jewish ownership of the *entire* Land of Israel. By spearheading a messianic "God will somehow solve it" approach to the large population of Arabs in the territories, they are willing to endanger the achievement of Jewish sovereignty for the cause of Jewish ownership. They say "all," but risk leaving the Jews with nothing.

Unfortunately, the success of Jewish maximalists in advancing their cause is due to their dependable allies: Arab maximalists and their collaborators. Arab maximalists are those who, at every historical moment they could have received "some," always repeated their mantra "all," only to be left with nothing. They are the ones who for more than a century repeatedly refused to accept that the Jews have a right to self-determination in at least some part of their homeland. They are the ones who rejected partition in 1947, because they wanted to do away with a Jewish state more than they wanted a Palestinian one. They are the ones who went to war over partition only to lose the war. They are the ones who kept the war going only to lose more territory in 1967. They are the ones who today claim to support two states while insisting that their "right of return" is "non-negotiable"—meaning they continue on their quest to destroy the Jewish state. They are the ones who use the language of "Palestinian rights" to deny that those "rights" are designed to deny the Jewish people their equal right to self-determination.

Israel's survival depends on Jews and lovers of Israel doing the same: fighting Jewish maximalists at home and fighting Arab maximalists abroad.

But Arab maximalists would not have had such success in advancing their cause had it not been for the Jewish maximalists. While the settlements are not the cause of the ongoing conflict—Arab maximalists have seen to that—they have obscured the foundational role of Arab maximalism in preventing a peace agreement that would acknowledge the permanence of the Jewish state. When messianic Jews repeatedly say, "it's all ours and only ours," it becomes much more difficult to name and shame the Palestinians for saying the same.

Unfortunately, Jewish and Arab maximalists have been successful at convincing those who could effectively do battle against them that to do so is impossible without serving the other side. As a result, those who feel that the survival of Israel and Zionism depends on defeating Jewish maximalists and their settlement project have, consciously or not, downplayed Arab maximalism. They have often been the first to hail Arabs "moderation" in denial of the facts on the ground. They have often excused Arab incitement, downplayed the Palestinians' attachment to their demand of "return," and treated persistent Arab maximalism and rejection of peace agreements as nothing more than a ruse used by Jewish maximalists to silence opposition.

Those who feel it necessary to defend Zionism by exposing Arab maximalism and defeating it have all too often found themselves pushed to unwillingly defend

Jewish maximalism, noting how Arab maximalists and their collaborators use settlements as the thin end of the wedge in their campaign to demonize Zionism and single out Israel in international forums. Dismayed by the way those purporting to fight against Jewish maximalism often fail to take any action against Arab maximalist claims, they naturally have little interest in playing into Arab maximalist hands, no matter how opposed they are to the settlements. Jewish maximalists, on their part, have used such occasions to rope those seeking to fight Arab maximalism into defending Jewish maximalism. I myself often had to put my foot down when some elements in the Israeli government tried to use my work fighting Arab maximalist claims to promote their Jewish maximalist agenda, which I oppose.

Yet the survival of Zionism has always depended on waging and winning wars on no less than two fronts. Today, Israel's survival depends on Jews and lovers of Israel doing the same: fighting Jewish maximalists at home and fighting Arab maximalists abroad with the same passion and vehemence. This should be the new standard for those who oppose both forms of maximalism. Jewish organizations that claim to promote a two-state solution should demonstrate that as much as they are fighting settlements, they are also fighting Arab maximalism. Jewish organizations that defend Israel and fight Arab maximalism shouldn't be afraid to take a stand against Jewish maximalists, if they wish to do so. Those among us who believe that a Jewish people that wants it all risks being left with nothing shouldn't have to choose their battles. We can save Zionism by defeating Jewish maximalists at home and Arab maximalists the world over.

The Tower
February 22, 2017

73

Peace Needs Constructive Specificity

From Ambiguity to Specificity

I am going to reflect on something central to the thinking of many policy-makers working to achieve peace. It is the notion that given the animosity, the distrust and the competing understandings of history, the way to make peace is through 'constructive ambiguity'. Shimon Peres, with whom I had a chance to work for a few years, used to say that 'in love-making, as in with peace-making, you need to close your eyes'. I'm not going to discuss people's preferences in the bedroom, but with respect to peace-making, I think that this

We now have two decades of experience with constructive ambiguity and it's clear that we should really call it destructive ambiguity. If we are to move forward what we need is constructive specificity.

perspective is not very helpful. The idea that we can close our eyes a little bit, that we can fudge the issues, that we can use words knowing that we understand those words one way and that the other side understands those same words in a completely different way – I think by now we have enough experience to know that this method is anything but constructive.

We now have two decades of experience with constructive ambiguity and it's clear that we should really call it *destructive* ambiguity. If we are to move forward what we need is constructive specificity. We need to be very clear about what we mean on the key components, on what makes peace possible and what it means to divide the land between the Jordan River and Mediterranean Sea into (to use the words of the UN) 'a Jewish state and an Arab state'. If we are to finally complete the partition, I believe that what is needed is for us to be very specific.

Constructive Specificity About the Border

What does constructive specificity mean? The first issue is the line of partition. Here we have a lot of words that are being used, such as 'the 1967 lines', 'pre-1967 lines', and in Israel talk of 'settlement blocs' and 'the barrier'. These kinds of words are, in the context of an agreement, used to describe where the border would be. But the time has come to be very specific about what we mean about the line of partition. When we say something like 'the 1967 lines with swaps', it is a good headline but it encourages both sides to continue to be unclear about where that line is. Everyone knows where the pre-1967 lines are, but once we introduce the idea of blocs and swaps it gets muddied.

The one thing that needs to happen, both in Israel and abroad – and this is something I am campaigning for, writing about and proposing that politicians take it as their agenda – is to actually put on the table a very clear delineation of Israel's final eastern border. I have published articles which list the settlements that Israel needs to include within its final eastern border and the ones it needs to exclude. The foreign ministries of Western countries interested in the conflict should do the same thing. Put a map on the table and begin to base a policy on this map. Say 'this is our working map of what we find acceptable'. We know what has undermined both American and EU foreign policy in the eyes of Israelis is that by failing to make a distinction between settlements that will be part of the state of Israel in a future agreement and those which will likely not be, the US and EU have not helped anyone's ability to fully understand what is needed to reach a final agreement.

I propose that the main blocs, except Ariel, should be part of Israel. Ariel goes too deep into the West Bank to be included. I propose that Ma'ale Adumim and Givat Zeev be connected to Israel only with a road. I propose four per cent of the territory of the West Bank, home to about 75 per cent of Israeli settlers, be annexed, with compensating swaps when a peace deal is agreed. Drawing a map would finally end the ambiguity. Once foreign offices in the West have a working map, they can begin to have a policy that is based on this map: much stricter on everything east of this line, but accepting of what is within the line, where building can continue. Policy would become wiser and more credible.

Constructive Specificity About Jerusalem

The second issue is Jerusalem. People mean different things when they speak of Jerusalem so, again, we need to be very clear. Jerusalem includes:

(a) The Jewish neighbourhoods west of the 1967 lines. Having grown up there I can assure you there is nothing holy or anything to get excited about in that part of Jerusalem. It is time for the world to be very clear that there is no question about the status of this part of Jerusalem. Moving western embassies to this part of Jerusalem should not be a big deal. It is time for the world to end the fiction that Jerusalem is an international protectorate to be governed by the world. It was an idea at the time of partition that, because of the war that followed, was never implemented. The time has come to stop toying with that fiction and to say instead 'we recognise that the Jerusalem West of the 1967 line is Israel'.

(b) The Jewish neighbourhoods built east of the 1967 line surrounding Jerusalem should be part of the map that would be put forward. For me, the Jewish neighbourhoods are part of the four per cent of territory, and 75 per cent of the population, that should be annexed to Israel, done in a way that would be minimalistic.

(c) The Arab villages which were not part of Jordanian East Jerusalem but were annexed to Jerusalem or included into the municipal boundaries after 1968. There is no question in my mind that these areas belong to the future Arab state. Again the world should be very clear that they do not recognise those areas as part of Israel, or Jerusalem, and that they should not be part of united Jerusalem.

(d) Finally there is the Old City. When people speak of Jerusalem they immediately think of the Western Wall, Temple Mount and al-Aqsa Mosque. However, that amounts to about 1 square kilometer; everything I have just discussed is nearly 100 square kilometers. So we have to be specific. About the Old City, we need to say that this is the only place where the controversy persists, so the status quo will continue, with an emphasis on ensuring access to the religious places until a decision is made on the final status of that square kilometer. The status of everything else can already be specified, and we would be in a much better position to agree on the status of the Old City if we do not let the ambiguity of that *part* spill over into the *whole*.

Constructive Specificity About Refugees

And finally I want to talk about the issue where I think there is the greatest need to be specific, and that is the refugees and the Right of Return. Amazingly, this is the core issue of the conflict from the Arab perspective, and they are still wedded to the maximalist vision that from the Mediterranean Sea to the Jordan River the state of Palestine will be free. Yet this is the area where the West is most blind. There is a term called 'mansplaining' – where men explain away what women have said because women are incapable of explaining something themselves – so I thought of introducing the idea of 'Westplaining' – the idea that Western countries explain away what Palestinians say. So when Palestinians say, 'we will return to Jaffa' or that they will 'never give up the Right of Return', that it is 'a personal right no leader can ever negotiate', and I have met with numerous Western diplomats whose countries donate to the authority that upholds those ideas, UNRWA, and they say to me 'but the Palestinians know they are not coming back, it's just a negotiating card for future talks'. This is not explaining but Westplaining

And this is why we need to be very specific. The Palestinians and the Arab world in general, as seen in the Saudi initiative, have come to use terms such as 'just' and 'agreed' to explain the solution to 'the refugee problem'.

However, these words are interpreted very differently by Arabs, by the West and by Israel. Regarding the term 'refugee' itself, by no other standard apart from UNRWA's would the five million Palestinians registered as refugees today be considered refugees. 80 per cent live west of the Jordan River and have never been displaced, or they are citizens of Jordan. We have an image of refugees as people who have just escaped from war, or who have lost their homes; we don't think of them as middle-class lawyers living in Ramallah. But this is what many Palestinian refugees are. So the term itself is deeply misleading and needs to be replaced.

The expression 'just and agreed' solution to the refugee problem is understood by many in the West and in Israel to mean that the Arab Palestinians will agree to compromise. But anyone who understands the details knows that if a Palestinian leader accepts the two-state solution and recognises Israel, whilst simultaneously insisting on the demand of return, then the only two-state solution they really support is an Arab state east of the Green Line now, and another Arab state west of the Green Line in the future. It means they have yet to accept the UN Partition Plan of an Arab state and a *Jewish* state. It is important to be specific: when the Arabs say a 'just' solution, they mean return. For them, justice is return. By contrast, the West and Israel think that 'just' means several possible solutions such as citizenship in Jordan, or a home in Canada.

Again, take the notion of 'agreed'. Many people think it means that what Israel does not agree to doesn't happen. But the Palestinian think of 'agreed' completely differently. It means agreeing now to what can be got – for example Israel accepting 5,000 Palestinian refugees a year

– while not dropping the demand for return. Palestinians emphasise that return is a personal right and that no leader can negotiate it away. What does this mean? It means that even if something is co-signed in an agreement, the demand will always exist. They can agree on a number today, but no agreement can end the demand for return due to the way that they have construed return.

Here, more than with any other issue, we need to be very specific. Israel and the West need to stop using terms like 'just' and 'agreed'. We have even heard officials like former US Secretary of State John Kerry use the words 'reasonable' and 'realistic'. The West and Israel think of a few thousand Palestinians returning as realistic; the Palestine papers demonstrated that the Arabs think Israel can absorb 2-3 million. The time has come to say: first, there has to be complete renunciation of the collective and individual Palestinian demand of a return west of the 1967 line, just as Israel needs to renounce Jewish return east of that border. It could be said that Israel, as a gesture, might allow 5,000 Palestinians to enter, but the numbers should be clear, and it will not be a right. Second, it needs to be clear that there is no legitimate claim to return. I understand that Palestinians will continue to dream of Palestine from the river to the sea – as some Jews may continue to dream of Judea – but there is a difference between people dreaming and the world supporting those dreams. Today, Jews who dream of Judea find themselves isolated in the world while Palestinians who demand Israel west of the 1967 lines do not. Because of the fudging of the words 'just,' 'agreed,' 'realistic,' and because of the continued financial support of the West to UNRWA, the Palestinians still think that they are supported in their maximalist claims rather than isolated.

Conclusion

Peace will be based on the understanding that both the Jews and the Palestinians are peoples indigenous to the land. Both have a serious claim to all of it, but if both insist on the exclusive and superior claim to it, it will be war forever. Peace depends on a clear renunciation by both sides of their exclusive claims, and a new understanding – that the other side's existence means they will only have some of the land. And the 'some' needs to be better defined. Even if both sides continue to have dreams, they need a far better understanding of how isolated they will become when those dreams make peace impossible.

Fathom
June 15, 2017

Yes to the Occupation, No to the Settlements

The developments have been many: the UN Security Council resolution declaring that the settlements have "no legal validity," the collapse of the Arab world, the rise of the right in Europe, and the election of Donald Trump in the United States, which has spurred on Israel's settler right wing. As a result, a golden opportunity has been created to secure Zionism's achievements for generations. This can be done through a policy of "yes to the occupation, no to the settlements," and with a bit of annexation, too.

This is the moment for anyone who wants to lead Israel, now or in the future, to draw a map, not mumble something about "two states," "settlement blocs," "the separation barrier" or "the 1967 lines with adjustments." Rather, we need a clear map showing Israel's eastern border and the limits of its territorial demands. West of the border will include annexed land where full citizenship is granted. To the east we need a policy of "yes to the occupation, no to the settlements."

The eastern border must be based on the required minimum to allow a significant number of settlers to join Israel, but no more than necessary. We must give up Ariel and correct the big mistake of annexing dozens of Palestinian villages to East Jerusalem after 1967; only Jewish neighborhoods would be included. This is only about 2 percent to 4 percent of the West Bank.

Anyone who publishes such a map must declare that the Jewish people and the State of Israel have a historical, legal and emotional right to the entire land between the Mediterranean Sea and the Jordan River, but this right is not supreme and exclusive.

It must be made clear that the Zionist movement recognizes the existence of another people that also views the land as its homeland. It has a right to this land, so we are willing to limit the fulfillment of our right to this territory. It must be stressed that the Zionist movement expects that at some stage the other side *The military occupation east of the border can be justified, the continuation of the settlements cannot.* must also limit the fulfillment of its right to the land, and that this right is not supreme or exclusive either.

The Arab Palestinian people must eventually lay down their arms against the Zionist movement, and in doing so recognize that the Jewish people have a right to a homeland in the Land of Israel. The Palestinians must therefore put limits on their demands for return or any other demand whose meaning is "Greater Palestine." Until this stage, Israel will continue to militarily hold territory east of the border.

Israel will accept any Palestinian entity that arises to the east of the border, whether a state or "autonomy on steroids" (as Education Minister Naftali Bennett has proposed). But only the Israeli army will be present on the ground. The occupation will continue.

Military occupation is an essential system of government in territories that are not intended to be annexed – until the end of a war. As long as Israel adopts a clear policy that proves its willingness to divide the land, the military occupation of these territories is justified until the other side proves a similar willingness.

So along with "yes to occupation," a policy of "no to settlements" will be declared. The military occupation east of the border can be justified, the continuation of the settlements cannot. There is no need for Security Council Resolution 2334 to understand that. A willingness to divide the land and recognize the right of another people to the land cannot exist alongside the settlement enterprise.

The "no" to the settlements must be unambiguous. There is no need to evacuate them, and there is no need for a compensation plan for those who leave. The settlements beyond the border should be left to wither economically and be deprived of support. Anyone who wants to live in these areas will do so without the support or protection of the Jewish sovereignty within its borders.

The result of this policy of "yes to occupation, no to settlements" will be the military occupation of the territory that will have a single legal system and a single population subordinate to this rule of law, without Israeli territorial demands and with a clear statement of the requirements to end the military occupation. Such a policy will achieve maximum separation between the two peoples and minimum friction.

To the west of the border a policy of full annexation and citizenship rights for everyone must be declared. The result will be a single system of justice – Israeli and equal for all. It will be clear who's inside and who's outside, who belongs and who doesn't.

A policy that sets a fair border with citizenship rights within this border is the political alternative to the messianic right. This policy recognizes the existence of another people between the Jordan River and the Mediterranean Sea but also recognizes that a long time will pass until this people agrees to the division of the land with the Jewish people.

This policy understands that land must be left for the other side, but Israel must remain militarily in the territory until its adversaries lay down their arms. This is a classic Zionist policy of exploiting geopolitical opportunities to forge major achievements, without the danger of messianic greed.

This is a return to Zionism's basic principles; people who take responsibility for their fate without waiting for the Messiah or God to solve their problems. It's the fulfillment of the Zionist tradition, the integration of a stirring vision and a pragmatic policy that operates according to the ancient Talmudic wisdom: If you grab too much you've grabbed nothing.

Haaretz
December 31, 2016

A Left-Wing Annexation Proposal

To counter the proposal of the settler right to annex Maale Edumim, the Israeli left should first put forth a proposal to annex Maale Edumim alone – and nothing else. To be more precise, the left should propose to annex Maale Edumim, the Jewish neighborhoods of East Jerusalem, as well as Har Adar, Har Homa, Givat Zeev, Gush Etzion, Beitar Illit, the suburbs of Modiin and the suburbs of Kefar Saba – and nothing else.

And if to be very precise – as it is about time – the left should propose to annex Ganei Modiin, Modiin Illit, Kefar Haoranim, Hashmonaim, Oranit, Alfe Menashe, Efrat, Elkanah, Shaarei Tikva, Har Adar, Beitar Illit, Elazar, Kefar Etzion, Alon Shevut, Rosh Tzurim, Neve Daniel, Bat Ain – and nothing else. In Jerusalem, the annexed neighborhoods should include French Hill, Maalot Dafna East, Kiryat Aryeh, Mivtar Hill, Ramat Eshkol, Ramot Allon, Ramat Shlomo, Giloh, Talpiot East, Pisgat Zeev and Neve Yaakov. The Arab villages, which were annexed to Jerusalem in a deeply mistaken historical decision, should be taken out.

With respect to the Old City of Jerusalem, the annexation proposal should call for the annexation of the Jewish Quarter, while maintaining the status of the rest of the Old City and the holy sites until a final peace agreement.

The annexation of Maale Edumim and Givat Zeev should include only the areas within those settlements that are built – not the extensive municipal borders, which include undeveloped areas. Furthermore, the annexation will include the road that connects the settlements to Jerusalem, and nothing more.

The total area of these annexed settlements is four percent of the total area of the West Bank, and home to seventy five percent of the Jewish citizens living there.

This annexation proposal must be accompanied with a declaration that the State of Israel is delineating its final eastern border and will have no further territorial demands with respect to the West Bank. The State of Israel will declare that upon a final peace agreement it will give the Palestinians other territories of equal size to those that were annexed.

The proposal must emphasize that the Jewish people have a deep historical and emotional connection to the territories beyond the border, but that the State of Israel recognizes that true peace compels both the Arabs and the Jews to accept that neither will have full ownership of the entire territory between the Jordan River and the Mediterranean Sea. The proposal will emphasize that from the time of the League of Nations Mandate, the State of Israel has had a legitimate legal claim to the territories; despite this legal claim, Israel will realize its right to only a minute portion of the land because of its commitment to peace through partition of the land between the two peoples laying claim to it.

Those who will take the initiative to put forth such an annexation proposal to the Knesset and the public will be able to end an extended period of mumblings about 'settlement blocks', vague interim proposals, and desperate calls for negotiations that at this moment cannot lead to a final peace agreement. The proposal will introduce into the Israeli discourse a clear political alternative that clarifies who is in and who is out. The proposal should also be presented to the U.S.

This annexation proposal must be accompanied with a declaration that the State of Israel is delineating its final eastern border and will have no further territorial demands with respect to the West Bank.

Administration, which seeks to understand Israel's intentions with respect to the territories. It will clarify that Israel has no intention to turn Ariel, Ofra, Beit El, Hebron and the rest of the mountain-top settlements into part of sovereign Israel, and that the people living there need to prepare for that.

The annexation proposal will also clarify that until a final peace agreement in which the Arab Palestinians recognize the equal right of the Jewish people to self-determination in the land of Israel, the Israeli Defense Forces will remain in the area between Israel's eastern border and the Jordan River; the military occupation will continue, but the settlement project will not. The Palestinian Authority will extend its civil authority to the entirety of the area which is not under Israeli sovereignty.

Israeli citizens who will remain in the area will receive military protection, but nothing more.

With the annexation of the settlements on the list, the State of Israel will cease all funding for settlements beyond its eastern border. It will not provide them with budgets, and will not fund government jobs. The settlers living there will be considered Israeli citizens living abroad. The only settlers who should receive compensation – if they choose to return to Israel within its borders – will be the residents of Ariel, who were subject to an ongoing presentation by the State of Israel that, despite their remote location, they belong to the 'settlement blocks' and are part of the 'consensus'.

This proposal will hand back the initiative to the Israeli left, that bereft of the ability to reach a final peace agreement with the Palestinians, has ceded the initiative entirely. It would enable the Israeli left to marshal support across the political spectrum. Based on this proposal, the Israeli left would be able to approach the settlers in the settlements listed for annexation, and tell them that while their leaders are peddling delusions of Area C annexation, this proposal could at the minimum achieve tacit American support, and thereby, once implemented, make the settlers living there proper citizens of the sovereign State of Israel.

Most important, this proposal would allow the Israeli left to stand – whether in elections or in the Knesset – against the efforts of the settler right to abuse the Israeli consensus with respect to the settlement blocks in order to promote an agenda of broad annexation – an annexation that even after fifty years, cannot muster the support of the majority of Israel's citizens, and for good reason.

EINAT WILF

Published in Hebrew by Haaretz
April 2, 2017

The Successful Disengagement

Twelve years ago, there was a disengagement that succeeded. It was the disengagement in northern Samaria. Many forget that the 2005 disengagement plan included, in addition to the Gaza strip, four isolated settlements in northern Samaria: Ganim and Kadim east of Jenin, and Humash and Sa-Nur south-west of Jenin, on the way to Nablus. During the planning process of the disengagement in the West Bank, the government of Israel decided not to choose four random settlements, but to remove four carefully selected ones that were all concentrated in the Jenin area. The isolated position of these settlements and their geographic concentration meant that, once removed, the entire Jenin district was without Israeli settlements and civilian Israeli presence.

The status of the northern Samaria territory was also maintained. Unlike Gaza, where Israel fully withdrew both the Israeli civilians and the military and turned over the entire territory to exclusive Palestinian control, the northern Samaria territory remained in C status – under full Israeli security and civilian responsibility. But unlike other

C areas, this one now had no settlements, and as a result of the disengagement legislation, Israeli citizens have not been allowed to enter the area without specific authorization from the military.

The outcome is that in northern Samaria the military occupation remains, but not the settlements. And it works: Jenin, the "suicide capital" during the bloody mayhem of the second Intifada, is now a calm and prosperous city. Jenin supplies nearly no terrorists, including during the recent waves of individuals attacks. The Palestinian residents in the Jenin area in all the sectors – A, B and C – enjoy lives, that even if not characterized by full political sovereignty, are mostly free of friction with various aspect of Israeli military control. As a result, on the Israeli side, the residents of Afula are not subject to the security threats typical of those living around Gaza, or even in Jerusalem.

The situation in northern Samaria is proof that if Israel removes isolated settlements in the midst of Arab population, while retaining operational freedom for the military, one can carry out a disengagement that does not end like Gaza and Southern Lebanon. Twelve years after disengagement, northern Samaria fulfills the promise of "we are here and they are there", while maintaining the security of Israel's citizens.

The northern disengagement is an unequivocal success, and for the annexationist right, that's a problem. The annexationist right seeks a security cover for its messianic annexationist schemes. It therefore prefers that when it comes to the future of the West Bank, the Israeli public will be under the mistaken impression that is faces only two alternatives: all or nothing, military occupation with settlements, or raining rockets on Ben Gurion and no settlers.

But there is another model for the future of the West Bank, and even a successful one – the civilians leave, the military doesn't. The northern Samaria disengagement proves that the choice does not have to be all or nothing. It is possible to say yes to the military presence and no to the civilian one. Israelis who insist on the right of Israeli citizens to security, and cast serious doubts over the benefits of a military withdrawal from the West Bank, don't have to be therefore recruited over to the cause of the settlements, and certainly not the ones not adjacent to the Green Line.

"Military-yes, Settlements-no" is the best current proven operational model.

The promotion of a political alternative to the annexationist right requires distinguishing the issue of Israel's freedom of military operation in the West Bank from the that of the presence of Israeli settlers, especially in areas not adjacent to the Green Line. The person who seeks to lead the political alternative to the annexationist right, should adopt the successful northern Samaria disengagement model and promote its implementation across the West Bank.

"Military-yes, Settlements-no" is the best current proven operational model that exists that secures Israel's citizens within the Green Line and in the adjacent settlements, and provides reasonable lives for the Palestinians in the West Bank. When the Palestinians finally and truly renounce their struggle against the equal right of the Jewish people to liberty and sovereignty in part of its ancient homeland, they will gain full sovereignty and liberty for themselves in the other part.

Co-Written with Shany Mor
Published in Hebrew by Haaretz
August 5, 2017

The Speech Ehud Barak Should Give

The place: Kefar Etzion

The time: Eve of elections

As I near my eightieth year I ask for the public's support in elections for one single purpose: to complete the partition of Israel into a Jewish state and an Arab state. The State of Israel has many challenges, but the struggle for a more just society, the fight against corruption and the healing of divisions, I leave to the leaders to come. I take upon myself one mission alone: the determination of final, clear, recognized and secure borders for the State of Israel.

My fellow settlers, on the morrow of my election to prime minister of Israel, I will annex to the State of Israel all of the settlements adjacent to the Green Line, where the vast majority of you live. Efrat and Tel Aviv, Kefar Etzion and Netanya will be equal towns in one State of Israel. This will become Israel's eastern border. This border is the outcome of your actions and settlement. We will be annexing a mere four percent of the entire territory of Judea and Samaria – less than one percent of the total territories conquered in the Six Day War. In their stead, following a final peace agreement, we will hand over to the Palestinians other territories of equal size

My fellow settlers, only I will be able to annex your settlements with the tacit agreement, if not more, of the governments of the United States, Europe, and the world at large. Only a leader who dared make peace, and is willing to do so again, will be able to complete what you have begun. Not Naftali Bennett, not Benjamin Netanyahu, and no other leader would be able to go to the world and say: we are annexing these settlements, and in doing so we have determined Israel's final eastern border. Only I can get for you that which you crave: recognition, legitimacy and belonging. At the end of my term you will no longer live under a cloud of impermanence and illegitimacy over your presence here.

My fellow settlers, I understand you. Unlike De-Gaulle, I am telling you the truth now, before the elections. East of the border that I have delineated before you, the State of Israel will have no territorial demands. The acts of settlement east of the border will cease, and will receive no support. Whoever lives east of the border could return to the State of Israel, within its borders, and will

> *Our responsibility as leaders is to make it easier, rather than harder, for future generations to make peace*

receive support for doing so. Whoever decides to remain, will be like any Israeli citizen who lives outside of Israel. The Palestinian Authority would be able to realize its authority over the entirety of the territory from the border to the Jordan River. The Jordan River will continue to be Israel's line of defense. The Israeli Defense Forces will retain freedom of action throughout the territories, as they do today. East of our final eastern border the military will stay, the citizens will not.

The late Supreme Court Justice Edmund Levy was right: we have a legal right to the territories of Judea and Samaria. Far more important, we have a deep historical and emotional connection to the lands of the Bible and the cradle of Jewish civilization – the home of the tribe and the Kingdom of Judea. We are an indigenous people who have come home. Nevertheless, there is another indigenous people in this land. Another people who have the equal right to be masters of their fate, determine their future, be sovereign, like all people. This land must be divided between the two peoples. In delineating our border, we will exhibit our ongoing commitment to the partition of the land between a Jewish State and an Arab State. We have a right to all of the land, but our right is neither exclusive, nor superior. We will not have all of the land. The dream of Greater Israel is over.

I call upon the Palestinians to abandon their dream of Greater Palestine as well. There will not be Palestine from the River to the Sea, just as there will not be Israel from the River to the Sea. I call upon the Palestinians to recognize the equal right of the Jewish people to self-determination in their homeland, just as we recognize the equal right of the Arab Palestinian people to self-determination in their homeland. I call upon the Palestinian refugees to recognize that the war is over, and that they and their millions of descendants will never return to the State of Israel within its borders. We will not return to Beit-El, Ofra and Hebron, east of our border, and the Palestinians will not return to Jaffa, Haifa and Magdal, west of the same border.

It is a tough demand, but peace requires tough and clear decisions. As long as the Palestinians continue their war for Greater Palestine, in the form of the demand for return, the Israeli Defense Forces will remain between our eastern border and the Jordan River. Full peace with the Palestinians may not be immediately attainable, but it does not mean we should do nothing. Our responsibility as leaders is to make it easier, rather than harder, for future generations to make peace. This is the responsibility I take upon myself.

The time has come for clarity and determination. I commit myself to leave to the leaders that follow me a state in which it is clear who is a citizen and who is not, a state that has completed the process of determining its borders, so that all the considerable capacities and energies of its citizens are turned towards building a more perfect society.

To this end I stand before you today, and with its completion, my decades-long service to the people and the State of Israel will be complete.

Published in Hebrew by Haaretz
November 19, 2017

Why Jerusalem Would Be Better Off Divided

I was born in Jerusalem after the Six-Day War, and spent my whole life living with the lie of its unification. Growing up in the capital in the 1980s and '90s, I knew there was no more transparent political lie than that of "the united city." This statement may have reflected the desires of certain Jerusalemites (and of some who didn't bother to live there), but it certainly had no relation to the reality of life.

The city was and remains divided. For us, its unification meant, at most, that – to the total consternation of our horrified parents – my girlfriends and I went into the Old City to buy sharwals. And while we did go to the "Old City" occasionally, we had absolutely no idea how to get to the Arab villages that were annexed to the city. It was also clear to everyone that these tens of villages – which hadn't even been part of Jordanian Jerusalem – may have been under the huge jurisdiction of the Jerusalem municipality, but there certainly wasn't any "unification" between Jerusalem as it was pre-1967 and these villages.

The desperate attempts to portray a united city were just that – desperate. The more it seemed that the last thing one could say about Jerusalem was that it was united, the more such official rhetoric escalated, and the more you saw Israeli leaders abroad shouting, "And Jerusalem is ours, united for all eternity!" as the crowds cheered.

When I listened to such speeches, all I could think was: Unity? Eternity? Are you kidding me?

People sought relief from all those lofty speeches by deflating the balloon a bit. A familiar joke around town in the '90s went: "Mayor Ehud Olmert has finally managed to realize the dream of his predecessor, Teddy Kollek, to unite the two parts of the city – now the western half is starting to look as neglected as the eastern part."

I clearly remember Jerusalem's descent into poverty and neglect, when the cost of maintaining the lie about unity swelled so high that it threatened to bury the city's residents.

I remember how Jerusalem went from being a magnet to an "outlying town" in need of ever-growing assistance just to keep the lie of its failed unification from being exposed. Growing up in the Beit Hakerem neighborhood in southwest Jerusalem, I remember how the neighbors gradually started moving out to Mevasseret Zion, and later to Modi'in. They didn't go as far as Tel Aviv. Even the massive building of new neighborhoods over the Green Line (the pre-1967 borders), and the network of roads and tunnels linking them to the western part of the city, didn't change the situation.

The city got bigger, poorer and uglier, and remained stubbornly divided. Granted, as Jerusalemites we sustained a proud local patriotism – that was part of the job description. But as we got older, many of us left the city, never to return.

As time went by, my experience of growing up in "united" Jerusalem spawned trepidation at the possibility that this city could be taken as a symbol of the nightmarish future of Israel as a whole: I'd seen with my own eyes what

Despite all the construction and tunnels, Jerusalem remains essentially divided.

happens when you annex too much territory in the name of an ideological lie. I'd seen how, partly due to this annexation, the two groups that reject Zionism – the ultra-Orthodox and the Arabs – were becoming the majority, while the creative and productive Zionist forces were fleeing to places where there was more openness and freedom, and less lying. And if Jerusalemites wanting to leave the city at least had the option of Tel Aviv, what would happen if the whole country was like that?

So, in the 1996 election, I paid careful attention to the statement that "Shimon Peres will divide Jerusalem," and wondered: Is that a threat or a promise? What's so great about united Jerusalem that we should fear its division?

After decades of living in the "united" city, it was obvious to me that the best thing that could happen to Jerusalem would be for it to be divided. That way, the city could direct its resources toward improving its economic situation and improving conditions for residents, rather than ongoing attempts to conceal the lie about its "united" existence.

I wasn't surprised when different groups of city planners and architects announced that, despite all the construction and tunnels, Jerusalem remains essentially divided – and that, therefore, it could be redivided into a Jewish city and Arab city, while preserving access to the Old City for anyone who wishes to go to the holy sites there.

One can actually imagine that it is possible to recreate Jerusalem anew, with its beating heart in the places that are the glory of Hebrew creation and Zionist sovereignty: the Knesset, the Supreme Court, the Israel Museum, the new National Library, the Hebrew University.

So on this Jerusalem Day, marking 50 years since the "unification" of the city, all I ask is that the next time a politician threatens to divide Jerusalem, they go ahead and do it.

Haaretz
May 25, 2017

Israel's Nation-State Bill Needs Borders

The deliberate vagueness of the bill's future geographic scope is at the base of the annexationist right's strategy: to advance a controversial agenda under a feigned cover of statesmanship and consensus

The Jewish nation-state bill needs a border. Not metaphorically, but in actuality. Before any constitutional questions about the nation-state bill come into consideration, the fundamental question is its geographic scope: Is the bill meant to be upheld solely in Israel within the Green Line (or at the most, within an adapted Green Line that includes minimal annexation of communities close to it), or is it meant to one day constitute a legal basis for a state that stretches from the Jordan River to the Mediterranean Sea?

Ostensibly, the nation-state bill, like any Israeli law, refers only to areas within the Green Line. But given that the promoters of the bill have always harbored a great fondness for the idea of annexing the Palestinian Territories, this is not at all certain. The deliberate vagueness of the bill's future geographic scope is at the base of the annexationist right's strategy: to advance a controversial agenda under a feigned cover of statesmanship and consensus.

The nation-state bill contains only one truly significant clause. This is the only basic section that is not open to broad and conflicting interpretations (What does Jewish mean exactly? What is "Israel's heritage"? What does special status of a language mean?) and has only one clear practical meaning: legislatively barring Palestinian self-definition. This section says: "The right to national self-definition in the State of Israel may only be exercised by the Jewish people."

At first glance, this might seem to be of little importance. "There's nothing there," some will say. This is the section that states that Israel is realizing the Jewish people's right to self-definition, as is written in the Israeli Declaration of Independence:

Israel within the Green Line enjoys a legitimacy around the world and among its own citizens, that is not the case for those who have settled beyond this line.

"This right is the natural right of the Jewish people to be masters of their own fate, like all other nations, in their own sovereign State." Other peoples can live in Israel as citizens but do not have the right to establish another nation-state within it.

If the nation-state bill were being advanced in tandem with a final determination of Israel's eastern border on the basis of an adapted Green Line, coupled with a declaration of an end to any territorial demands east of this border, one could rightly argue that at such a momentous time, when a decisive step is being taken toward dividing the land between a Jewish state and an Arab state, the Jewish people's unique right to self-definition – within these Israeli borders – should be anchored in law, along with full civil equality for all.

There is a possibility – by no means negligible – that the nation-state bill is designed to lay the legal groundwork for one state that covers the entire area between the Jordan River and the Mediterranean Sea. In this context, the bill aims to decide the basic political question in Israel by stipulating that a Palestinian state, or state-minus (autonomy), or any other form of Palestinian Arab self-definition between the Jordan and the sea, will not come into existence – ever. This means that this state, a large portion of which – possibly even a majority – will be Arabs, will be defined in the constitution as a Jewish state in which Arabs do not enjoy equality, either national or civil. And that is not nothing. That is practically everything.

In spite of all of its efforts, the annexationist right is well aware that while the Israel within the Green Line enjoys a legitimacy around the world and among its own citizens, that is not the case for those who have settled beyond this line – especially when they've settled deep in the territories. Thus, for decades, and particularly in recent years, the annexationist right has been desperately trying to get some of the legitimacy of Israel within the Green Line to rub off on what is beyond it, so that when the time comes, opposition to annexation of the territories will be diminished.

This explains a ceremony to celebrate the settlements in Gush Etzion, under a false mantle of an "official" state event. This explains a bill that could serve as a basis for annexation of the territories – while denying people who live there all individual and collective rights – will be advanced by attacking its opponents as "eager to recognize a Palestinian nation-state and adamantly opposed to a Jewish nation-state," as Netanyahu put it.

Many cannot easily point to substantive sections of this bill that they oppose, but because they can smell hidden intentions here, they object and say things like, "It's unnecessary" or "It's harmful" or "A constitution is not needed." For the most part, these are justified and correct arguments, but they fail to expose the annexationist right's strategy of feigning no untoward motives ("So you're against a Jewish state?"; "Only the Arabs deserve rights?"; "A state is fine for the Palestinians but not for the Jews?"). So the proper, and politically wise, response to the annexationist right's attempt to use the nation-state bill to further advance its vision of one state between the river and the sea in which only the Jews enjoy national and civil rights is: You know what? Fine, you can go right ahead with a nation-state law – as long as you create a border too.

Haaretz
October 8, 2017

IV. ON WHAT THE INTERNATIONAL COMMUNITY SHOULD DO

For those who actually care about understanding, and perhaps one day, resolving the conflict, it is worth keeping in mind that the conflict between Israelis and Palestinians, between Jews and Arabs in the Middle East, rests on serious issues that go to the core of matters of each other's sense of justice, history, and identity. Most important to bear in mind, is that Israelis, Palestinians, and Arabs are sovereign agents who need to determine their future for themselves and by themselves. This means that no-one – no matter how spiritual and saintly – can do it for them, even if he or she believe that resolving this specific conflict is the burden they have been charged with by God. They have not.

Fathom
Autumn 2017

If the word peace is ever to truly describe the situation between Israel and its neighbors, it requires the Arab and Muslim world to address the roots of their intolerance. It requires them to accept the Jews as their equals and as an indigenous people who have come home. This was always too large a task to be undertaken by the Palestinians. Only Arabs and Muslims together can legitimize a different theological interpretation of the Jewish presence in their midst: no longer inferiors and no longer foreigners. In doing so, they can enable and legitimize practical solutions in Jerusalem that accept the centrality of the city to the Jewish people, and to the manufactured problem of the "refugees", by finally rehabilitating them and absorbing them as fellow Arabs.

Co-Written with Adi Schwartz
The Hill
February 24, 2017

Oslo | Staging the 'White Man's Burden'

The play *Oslo* which opens at the Lyttleton Theatre in London on 5 September, is ostensibly about peace. In reality, it is a thinly disguised variation on the theme of 'The White Man's Burden'. The play is not – as one might expect – about how Israelis and Palestinians came together in 1993 to forge an agreement intended to bring about peace over time. Rather, it is about how altruistic Norwegians were able to civilise, albeit only partially, two primitive warring tribes, that until the white man's (and woman's) saintly intervention, knew no better than to engage in senseless violence.

Multiple elements convey this message throughout the play: Israeli and Palestinian characters are portrayed as cartoonish stereotypes that emphasize their 'otherness'; whatever issues underlie their conflict are mocked and dismissed; the violence between the sides is a decontextualised endless cycle with no reason; and the Norwegian diplomats – true to Norway's historic standing as the world's top exporter of Christian missionaries per capita – are on a mission from God. The bottom line, by the play's end, is that 'the white man and woman' tried their best, but there is a limit to what one can do with brutes.

The crass stereotypes of Israeli and Palestinian characters were my first clue that something was deeply wrong with the play. When I recently saw *Oslo* in New York at the Lincoln Center Theater, being a member of one of the warring tribes, I was shocked by its portrayal of people with whom I worked closely and knew well – Yossi Beilin, Uri Savir, Yair Hirschfeld and Ron Pundak. Beilin and Savir are presented as foul mouthed Israeli thugs – in what is about the furthest possible characterisation from who they are. The weighty and serious Hirschfeld and Pundak are portrayed as early Woody-Allen type bumbling Jews. It is as if in coming to represent Israeli Jews, the only two possibilities the director could imagine were very Jewishey Jews or Israeli thugs. Granted, a more accurate portrayal of all four of them as the bureaucratic and academic nerds that they are could have robbed the play of some of its dramatic appeal, but one wonders if there shouldn't be a way to satisfy dramatic needs without resorting to demeaning shortcuts. (It is perhaps no accident that the one Israeli who is portrayed as he is, is Shimon Peres, who is far too well known to mess around with.)

The Arab characters, Ahmed Qurie and Hassan Asfour, were subjected to a similar stereotypical portrayal. They are loud mouthed, uncouth, with Asfour in particular, presented as the caricature of an Arab communist – with every one of his utterings a ridiculous speech. Asfour's portrayal serves two purposes; to present him as an Arab 'other,' and to mock his communism, the ideology most inimical to any Christian missionary. Not for a moment is the possibility entertained that communism played an important and legitimate role in the forging of a post-colonial Arab identity.

In general, the possibility that serious ideas, interests and ideologies underlie the conflict, is noticeably absent from the play. To judge from the script, Israelis and Palestinians don't have any real issues that explain the tenacity of the conflict. Instead it offers us a cauldron in which words like 'terrorism,' 'colonialism,' 'gassed grandparents,' and 'Jerusalem' arouse emotions, for no apparent reason. Violence is senseless and cyclical; whenever violent events off-stage are referred to in the play, it is in a monotonous recital of 'A murdered B,' 'B retaliated,' 'A rioted'.

This disregard for the issues that actually underpin the conflict is displayed in a telling scene in which Savir and Qurie, upon their first negotiation meeting, tell each other how their respective people's views the other ('terrorists', 'murderers'). Once each is done with his lurid expose, the character of Savir sums this exchange as, 'Well, now that we've both swung our dicks.' To the writer, who put these words in the character Savir's mouth, the conflict between Israelis and Palestinians is essentially a form of 'swinging dicks' – the very image of a primitive tribal ritual.

And who saves these primitive tribes, engaged in a contest of 'swinging dicks,' from their endless and senseless cycle of violence? The 'white man' of-course, who, in this play, is embodied in the form of the two married Norwegian diplomats, Tarje Larsen and Mona Juul, an almost Maria-like figure.

The civilising mission of the diplomats is expressed in a scene in which Larsen and Juul undertake to calm down the savages. In the only expression of actual violence on the stage, which is, true to stereotypes, by an Arab, Qurie nearly hits Larsen. His violent outburst, well into the play, underscores that despite the civilising process he has undergone so far, and the grand Norwegian palace exterior, the savage remains underneath.

Israelis, Palestinians, and Arabs are sovereign agents who need to determine their future for themselves and by themselves.

The following scene encapsulates the condescending undertone of the entire play. Like a young chided boy, Qurie appeals to Juul to make amends for his behaviour. In response, she motions to him, as if he were a five-year old, to make friends and go for a walk with his Israeli negotiating partner, Savir. Qurie tries to wiggle out of this unpleasant chore, but like a stern mother, Juul will have none of it. So, chastised, the two infants Qurie and Savir go for a walk in the woods under the watchful eye of the Norwegian diplomats. As Savir and Qurie begin to engage in friendly conversation, Larsen and Juul look on pleased and proud, as if they were just able to happily resolve a playground crisis between two annoyingly rowdy children.

This scene also caters to one of the central premises of the Norwegian civilising mission, which is, that by forging personal relations and creating 'bonds of trust' between negotiators, peace can be made and ancient enmities overcome. During their conversation in the woods, Savir and Qurie share a smoke and learn that their daughters have the same name – Maya. This is a pregnant moment. The audience learns that both Israeli and Palestinian men can be fathers! That both can have daughters named Maya! Hey, so these brown people are indeed similar! Which means that what they're fighting over can't be serious! And peace is just around the corner! Hurrah! So, all that is needed for making peace between Jews and Arabs, Israelis and Palestinians, is for them to just get to know each other and see that their differences don't amount to a hill of beans in this world. Indeed, given that Israelis and Palestinians don't have any real substantive issues that merit serious consideration, the key to forging an agreement between them, according to Larsen, is the application of 'constructive ambiguity' – essentially, diplomatic high speak for fudging the issues. And the issues can be fudged, since they aren't that important anyway.

But everything is excused for the diplomats, because their motivations are altruistic and entirely noble. In a most telling interaction well into the play, one of the Israeli negotiators turns to Juul to ask her, 'Why are you doing this?' He wants to know why a Norwegian diplomat has decided to devote her time to an issue that does not directly affect her. It is a wholly legitimate and reasonable question from someone who actually has a stake in the issue. Especially given that he, unlike her, would not be able to run away to the comforts of northern Europe when everything later will literally blow up in his face.

The answer of Juul to this straightforward question? 'If you have to ask, you wouldn't understand my answer.' Herein lies the message of the entire play: the warring tribes are incapable of fathoming the spiritual mission that guides the Norwegian diplomats. All that the tribesman can comprehend is people contending themselves with their immediate earthly concern. They cannot understand why the 'white man' would spend time and effort making peace between warring tribes living thousands of miles away. The tribesmen cannot grasp that the Norwegian is animated by a higher spirit and a noble goal. In fact, the 'white man and woman' are so noble that they can't even bother to communicate their higher spiritual mission to the lowly tribesman – as he 'wouldn't understand'. Indeed, the 'white man' is so willing to sacrifice himself for the good of humanity, that when it becomes clear that Juul and Larsen would not be seated at the honorary tables following the signing of the accords, the saintly Juul/Maria reminds Larsen that 'it is not about us'.

Alas, when, by the end of the play, it becomes clear that the warring tribes have descended yet again to their endless cycle of senseless violence, Larsen turns to the audience to assess his handiwork. One would think, that given the time that has passed and the spectacular failure of it all, the diplomat would have to answer for the complete collapse of his two key premises – that constructive ambiguity contributes to peace-making, and that personal relations can overcome deep seated enmities. But no, rather than admit that constructive ambiguity has been a disaster, and that personal relations, while nice, cannot replace the deep forces that drive the conflict, the character of Larsen invokes the audience to 'not look at where we are,' but to 'see how far we have come' (how far, really?). He might as well have asked the audience to 'not judge the tribes by the fact that they still can't play cricket, but celebrate the fact that they can hold a knife and fork'.

Oslo might be a well written play that keeps up the dramatic pace of what is supposedly a serious and heavy issue. But for those who actually care about understanding, and perhaps one day, resolving the conflict, it is worth keeping in mind that the conflict between Israelis and Palestinians, between Jews and Arabs in the Middle East, rests on serious issues that go to the core of matters of each other's sense of justice, history, and identity. It also so happens that these two warring tribes are engaged in a conflict no more violent (and in fact a whole lot less) than other conflicts raging around the world (and certainly *much* less violent than those conducted by 'white men' over the centuries); that moving towards peace requires constructive specificity that directly and clearly addresses the most contentious issues; and that personal relations among negotiators make for a nice atmosphere, but can't replace the larger forces that drive the conflict. Finally, and most important to bear in mind, is that Israelis, Palestinians, and Arabs are sovereign agents who need to determine their future for themselves and by themselves. This means that no-one – no matter how spiritual and saintly – can do it for them, even if he or she believe that resolving this specific conflict is the burden they have been charged with by God. They have not.

Fathom
Autumn 2017

A Very Big Deal to Solve a Very Big Problem

President Donald Trump, as expressed in the press conference with Israeli Prime Minister Netanyahu, now aspires in the Middle East to "a much bigger deal", "a much more important deal", one that "would take in many, many countries" and "would cover a very large territory." This kind of regional deal between the Arab world – and perhaps, the entire Muslim world - and the Jewish State of Israel was always the only deal to be had: a very big deal to solve a very big problem.

True peace requires addressing the deep sources of the conflict. Those lay with the Arab and Muslim reaction to the return of the Jewish people to powerful sovereignty in their ancient homeland. As far as Muslim theology and Arab practice were concerned, the Jews were non-believers, only to be tolerated, never as equals. They should have never been allowed to undermine Muslim rule over the lands, which the Jews claimed as their homeland, but the Arabs viewed as exclusively theirs since conquering them in the seventh century.

The return of the Jewish people to restored sovereignty in their ancient homeland, required Arabs and Muslims to accept that a people, whom they have for centuries treated as inferiors, worthy of contempt, were now claiming equality and exercising power in their midst.

This historical "Chutzpah" is what drove the Arab League to violently reject any kind of plan that would grant the Jewish people equal sovereignty over

The Palestinians have been at the forefront of Arab and Muslim intolerance, but they are not its creators.

any part of "Muslim land", free from their control. This unnatural historical development, in Arab eyes, led Arab governments to take revenge and forcefully expel hundreds of thousands of Jews, living in their midst, often in communities predating the birth of Islam, just after the establishment of the State of Israel.

It is also the reason why Arab states kept the Arabs who were displaced during the 1948 Arab-Israeli war and their millions of descendants, as perpetual "refugees" – to deprive the Jewish state of legitimacy and peace. It is the reason that even after losing repeated military wars against the State of Israel, Arab countries have continued their diplomatic and economic war against it to this day. Even Jordan and Egypt, that have signed nominal peace agreements with Israel, have more of a 'mutual non-attack' agreements, rather than genuine peace.

The animosity to the concept of the Jewish sovereignty in the Arab Middle East is simply too big. This attitude towards the Jewish state is an Arab – and Muslim – issue, and not only a Palestinian one. The Palestinians have been at the forefront of this Arab and Muslim intolerance, but they are not its creators. They are the thin end of the wedge by which the Arab and Muslim world wages its war against a sovereign Jewish people.

If the word peace is ever to truly describe the situation between Israel and its neighbors, it requires the Arab and Muslim world to address the roots of their intolerance. It requires them to accept the Jews as their equals and as an indigenous people who have come home. This was always too large a task to be undertaken by the Palestinians. Only Arabs and Muslims together can legitimize a different theological interpretation of the Jewish presence in their midst: no longer inferiors and no longer foreigners. In doing so, they can enable and legitimize practical solutions in Jerusalem that accept the centrality of the city to the Jewish people, and to the manufactured problem of the "refugees", by finally rehabilitating them and absorbing them as fellow Arabs.

This is a tall order, and therefore only a powerful nation, such as the United States, can create the conditions for such an agreement. This means continuing and even enhancing the American multi-layered support for Israel, so as to disavow any people or nation of the possibility of doing away with the State of Israel. But it also means finally addressing the Arab attitudes towards the Jewish state. The problem is that for decades, the U.S. went along with Arab duplicity, and even enabled it. Washington treated several Arab governments as its allies, while allowing them to foster and spread anti-Israeli hatred. It is time for the new administration to put its money where its mouth is: if the U.S. is serious about achieving a "great deal", it should start exacting a price on any Arab behavior contrary to that end.

There is a range of actions that the U.S. can take. In any statement regarding the conflict, the new administration must acknowledge that Arab animosity towards the sovereign Jewish state is the root cause of the conflict. The U.S. should put an end to its policy of providing Arab countries a carte blanch for not resettling the refugees for nearly seventy years, and cease financially underwriting this behavior through the American decades-long support of a special UN agency (UNRWA). The U.S. should also put a price tag on any Arab anti-Israeli activity in the UN and in international fora. The U.S. could also exact a financial price on the continued Arab and Muslim economic boycott of Israel as well as its boycott in a variety of fields from soccer to culture.

By doing so, the U.S. would send an unequivocal message to the Arab and Muslim world that their future is better served by accepting Israel and the Jewish people as sovereign and equal in their midst, rather than by continuing the useless war they have been waging against Israel, Zionism and the sovereign Jewish people.

Co-Written with Adi Schwartz
The Hill
February 24, 2017

The U.N. Can Find Balance in the Middle East

The United Nations Security Council last month passed Resolution 2334, which states that Israeli settlements have "no legal basis." The resolution made the mistake of only looking at one side of the map. To complete the job, the U.N. should pass a resolution that condemns Palestinian maximalist claims with the same sharp legal language it used for Israeli claims. In the absence of that, the U.N. resolution and the coming Paris peace conference will do more harm than good to the prospects of peace and justice.

Resolution 2334 forcefully reasserted the 1949 Armistice line—also known as the pre-1967 line or Green Line—which separates the West Bank from the state of Israel. The resolution took great pains to delineate the lines in clear language. It called the entire territory east of that line "Palestinian Territory." It then asserted that the establishment of Israeli settlements in that territory had "no legal validity and constitutes a flagrant violation under international law."

The resolution also said that it will not "recognize any changes" to the lines, "other than those agreed by the parties through negotiation." Contradicting U.N. Resolution 242 from 1967, it essentially gave all the land to the Palestinians and took away from Israel all leverage in future negotiations. It called upon all member states "to distinguish, in their relevant dealings, between the territory of the State of Israel and the territories occupied since 1967."

The Security Council should send an equally forceful message to Palestinians. If Israelis cannot lay claim to Palestinian territory, then Palestinians cannot lay claim to Israeli territory. Secretary of State John Kerry and participants of the coming peace conference in Paris must affirm such a resolution as strongly as they did the U.N.'s original one.

If Israelis cannot lay claim to Palestinian territory, then Palestinians cannot lay claim to Israeli territory.

Conventional wisdom has it that the Palestinians have long ago abandoned their claims to Israel west of the Green Line. But those who have witnessed the chants of "from the river to the sea, Palestine will be free" at anti-Israel demonstrations know how wrong conventional wisdom can be.

The most flagrant manifestation of these Palestinian claims is the insistence that the Arabs who were displaced during the 1947-49 war, and their millions of descendants, possess a "right of return" to the state of Israel. Palestinian Authority President Mahmoud Abbas and his foreign minister have both expressed support for this position. Yet to insist on this "right" means to deprive the Jewish people of their state and subject them again to the status of an oppressed minority—their historical position in Arab lands. It means that when the Palestinian Arabs speak of the two-state solution, while still calling for the "right of return," they are effectively calling for the establishment of two Arab states.

A new resolution must be clear that Palestinians do not possess a "right of return" to anywhere but east of the pre-1967 lines, in the "Occupied Palestinian Territory," as Resolution 2334 describes them. Those already living in those areas cannot lay any claim to "return" to Palestine, as they are already there.

Particularly, the resolution should affirm, using the same language as Resolution 2334, that any claims of Palestine and of Palestinians to the territory of Israel within the 1967 lines have "no legal validity" and "constitute a flagrant violation under international law." Any institutions perpetuating such claims, such as U.N. Relief and Works Agency for Palestine Refugees in the Near East, should "immediately and completely cease" their illegal activities and be dismantled. Any changes, such as enabling more Arab Palestinians to become citizens of Israel, will not be recognized "other than those agreed by the parties through negotiation." All member states should be called to "distinguish between Palestine and Palestinians in the territories occupied since 1967 and any Palestinians claiming any rights beyond those territories."

If backers of the original resolution decline to use the same language toward the Palestinians that they used against Israelis, then those who doubt their commitment to peace and justice would, unfortunately, be vindicated.

Co-Written with Adi Schwartz
The Wall Street Journal
January 13, 2017

123

The Green Line Strikes Back

The Green Line has returned with a vengeance. Decades of efforts to erase it have come to naught. If United Nations Security Council Resolution 2334, Secretary of State John Kerry's subsequent speech, and Sunday's Paris peace conference have proven anything, is that the Green Line has struck back.

That's a good thing.

The Green Line, commonly referred to as the June 1967 line and more precisely referred to as the 1949 armistice line, separates the West Bank from the State of Israel. But more importantly, it separates the Zionism that built the country from the Zionism that could destroy it. The return of the Green Line in international discourse is an opportunity to revive the much-needed debate between Zionism-of-the-people and Zionism-of-the-land, between secular Zionism and messianic Zionism, between the original Zionism of sovereignty and the later, mutated Zionism of idolatry.

Zionism was the movement of a people who sought their liberation by becoming masters of their own fate. It was not the movement of a people who wanted to become slaves to a land. Zionism was born so that the Jewish people would be free in a land of their own, but not so they would own the land in its entirety. The reason that the Zionist movement was so remarkably successful in achieving its goals was precisely due to its laser-sharp focus on sovereignty rather than land; so much so that to attain a state for the Jewish people that was sanctioned by the United Nations, the Zionist leadership was willing to accept a partition plan that allowed for the creation of a Jewish state without Jerusalem—without the Zion in Zionism—and without Judea, the last place where Jewish sovereignty reigned.

The Green Line separates the Zionism that built the country from the Zionism that could destroy it.

In terms of examples of historical leadership, this decision of the Zionist movement to accept partition, and to avoid the trap of messianic greed, could count as miraculous. Had the Zionist leadership dropped the ball on its supreme goal of sovereignty, the Jewish people would have probably had neither liberty nor land. Moreover, the moral courage of the Zionist leadership in saying "I do" to 54 percent of the land between the Jordan River to the Mediterranean Sea (most of it desert), even though it was promised 100 percent by the League of Nations, stood out against the Arab maximalist demand of 100 percent. This stance was rewarded when, at the end of the 1948-1949 war, the state of Israel was recognized by many of the world's nations on territory comprising 78 percent of the land—that is, the territory within the armistice lines. By saying yes to less, Israel gained more. By saying all or nothing, the Arabs were left with nothing.

This ancient Talmudic lesson that was demonstrated so exquisitely by the divergent Zionist and Arab responses to partition—*tafasta meruba lo tafasta* (try to grab too much and you'll be left with nothing)—has been lost on the messianic settler movement. For several decades now, the movement has sought to erase the distinction between the state of Israel and the land of Israel. By settling in the territories that Israel captured in the 1967 Six-Day War, and especially by doing so under the mantle of religion, it sought to refashion Zionism as a movement that is a about the land of Israel rather than the people of Israel.

A message for those who imagined that the settlers were successful in their cause—whether they were pleased or concerned by it—came in the form of last month's Security Council resolution, which resurrected with force the 1949 armistice lines. It reminded those in Israel, and those outside it who have been taken by the ideological fervor of the settler movement, that the movement is bereft of international support. By taking such great pains to emphasize that all that is beyond the Green Line does not belong to Israel, the resolution essentially affirmed what *does* belong to Israel. The resolution, even if this was not the intention, gives international sanction to the Zionism that created Israel within the Green Line—the secular Zionism of a people seeking nothing more than their liberty and equality among the nations. By condemning the settlements so harshly, the resolution powerfully rejected the post-1967 mutation of Zionism by the settlers into a Messianic religious movement that subjects a people to the false idolatry of land and greed.

There is nothing sacrosanct in the 1949 armistice lines, but in the absence of the State of Israel delineating a clear border within the West Bank that puts a final limit on its territorial claims, the Green Line has become the line that distinguishes the kind of Israel that the world is willing to support from the kind that it is not. Even if unintended, the events of the past month have been a powerful affirmation of the remarkable achievements of secular Zionism, and a warning sign of the dangers of greed. It gives an opportunity to all of us who are heirs to that original Zionist vision, to proudly say: We are privileged to be free and sovereign in the land of our ancestors, and we do not need to own every part of it to know that we are of it.

The Tower
January 17, 2017

A How-To Guide for Moving the U.S. Embassy to Jerusalem

To the President of the United States, attached please find a short four-step how-to guide for moving the American embassy in Israel from its present location in Tel Aviv, Israel's cultural and economic capital, to Jerusalem, Israel's political capital. This guide will enable you, the President, to realize a clear campaign promise, support an ally, stand by those truly committed to justice and peace, end a longstanding but entirely nonsensical U.S. policy, and, as a cherry on top, expose hypocrisy.

Step 1:

Choose a location for the embassy in Jerusalem that is clearly west of the 1949 armistice line, also known as the 1967 line. This part of Jerusalem has been under undisputed Israeli sovereignty since there was a modern state of Israel. This part has nothing holy in it -- it is humdrum neighborhoods (I know, I grew up there). Make a special effort to find a location that overlooks the most important sites in this part of the city, all conveniently located next to each other: the Israeli Knesset, the

Make it clear in your statements that the move merely acknowledges what has been known for decades.

Supreme Court, the government offices, the Hebrew University, and the new National Library. You will note that these are proud symbols of the achievement of Israel and Zionism, symbols of Israeli sovereignty, knowledge, and creativity. You could do no better than place the symbol of the friendship between our two countries in their proximity.

Don't be tempted to place the embassy in the area that was the no-man's land before 1967, where some claim land has already been purchased for that purpose, and certainly nowhere east of the 1967 lines. This might not completely satisfy Jewish maximalists, but it is critical for the success of this move and for the ability to reach the above goals, especially the hypocrisy exposure one.

Step 2:

Make it clear in your statements that the move merely acknowledges what has been known for decades -- the parts of Jerusalem west of the 1967 line undisputedly belong to Israel, and Israel has the sovereign right of every nation to place its capital in its undisputed territory. Add that this move will finally put to bed the fiction that the vast area that encompasses Jerusalem west and east of the 1967 line is a "Corpus Separatum" -- a separate entity -- that belongs to the international community, as envisioned in the UN 1947 partition proposal. This fiction, as all good fictions do, never existed anywhere but on paper. It never existed for the simple reason that the Arabs rejected the partition proposal and opened war to prevent it from being realized, and in losing the war Jerusalem west of the armistice lines became undisputedly Israel's, and Jerusalem east of the line entered an extended period of disputed claims.

Clarify that nearly seventy years after the end of that war, the United States is finally ending an illogical policy that holds the undisputed status of Jerusalem west of the 1949 armistice line hostage to the ongoing dispute over Jerusalem east of that line. The United States is done denying Israel a basic national sovereign right to establish its capital in undisputed territory. You can add a statement that the United States continues to call upon Israelis and Palestinians to directly negotiate the future of Jerusalem east of the 1967 line, with a special call that any arrangement should be mindful of the importance of the holy places, found only in Jerusalem east of the 1967 lines, to Judaism, Christianity, and Islam and secure freedom of access and worship to these sites.

This should minimize the threat of violence in response to the move since such statements would give Palestinians, Arabs, and Muslims who are not opposed to Israel within the 1967 lines a face-saving hook that would allow them to treat the U.S. move as changing nothing, and therefore not deserving of a negative response.

Step 3:

Call out those Palestinians, Arabs, and Muslims who are threatening violence over the U.S. move for their real meaning: are they denying that Jerusalem west of the 1967 line clearly belongs to Israel? Are they laying claim to that territory too? After decades of asking the world to limit Jewish and Israeli claims east of the 1967 line, are they demanding Israel west of that line for themselves as well? If Palestinians, Arabs, and Muslims oppose the U.S. move, as outlined above, they are essentially saying that Israel even within the 1967 lines is illegitimate, and thereby expose their enduring maximalist claims.

As a longstanding supporter of the Palestinian right to self-determination, I have found that it is critical that Palestinian, Arab, and Muslim maximalists should be called out for what underlies their fury: nothing less than racism plain and simple, a continued denial that the Jewish people, no more and no less than any other people, possess the equal and universal right for self-determination in their land. While those Palestinians, Arabs, and Muslims might react with violence, it is a violence that is based not on opposition to the move itself, but on a more base opposition to the very existence of the state of Israel. This is an important opportunity to clarify that America will not bow to that, and neither should any other country.

Step 4:
Call upon all other countries that have diplomatic relations with Israel to follow suit. Address your call especially to those countries that voted for UN Security Council Resolution 2334, that so thoroughly denied Jewish and Israeli claims east of the 1967 line, as well as to those countries who participated in the Paris Conference, which affirmed the resolution. Their resolution, even if unintended, powerfully affirmed that there is absolutely no legal dispute or claim to Israeli territory west of the 1967 lines, including in Jerusalem. This legitimate interpretation of the language of the resolution provides sufficient legal basis for moving the embassy to Jerusalem west of the 1967 lines. Make it clear that the United States will view as utter hypocrisy any country denying Jewish and Israeli

claims east of that line while refusing to take the most obvious step to acknowledge the undisputed nature of Israeli territory west of that line.

There you have it Mr. President, a clear and simple path to achieving a multitude of goals: swiftly realizing a major campaign promise, demonstrating your friendship to a longstanding ally, shaking stale Beltway orthodoxies, standing up to maximalists and hypocrites alike, and actually taking a real step toward justice and peace for Israelis and Palestinians. Good luck.

The Washington Institute
January 30, 2017

Finally, a President Who Looks at Jerusalem Logically

President Trump was correct when he said Wednesday that recognizing Jerusalem as Israel's capital is "nothing more nor less than a recognition of reality—it is also the right thing to do." In fact, the U.S. decision to recognize Jerusalem as Israel's capital is 68 years overdue.

Jerusalem was established as the capital of the newly independent state of Israel on December 13, 1949. This was Jerusalem west of the ceasefire line delineated at the end of the war for Israel's independence, later to be known as the pre-1967 line. This part of Jerusalem included Jewish residential neighborhoods built in preceding decades. There was nothing holy about this

The U.S. decision to recognize Jerusalem as Israel's capital is 68 years overdue.

part of Jerusalem. By the end of the war the holy and ancient sites were actually east of the ceasefire line: the entire Old City, including the sites holiest to the Jewish people. The Temple Mount, the Wailing Wall, and the Jewish Quarter all came under Jordanian control, and Jews were denied access to these sites.

The United States recognized the State of Israel upon its independence, so it should have been straightforward for the U.S. to recognize Jerusalem as Israel's capital and to establish its embassy there. If anything, it is the Jordanian annexation of the Old City and the way Jews were denied access that should have led to international consternation (it didn't).

Why didn't the U.S. and all other countries recognize residential, non-holy, west-of-the-armistice-line Jerusalem as Israel's capital? At the time, the U.S. was still attached to an idea, proposed in the United Nations partition resolution of 1947, that the vast area of greater Jerusalem (including residential neighborhoods) as well as Bethlehem should be a "Corpus Separatum," a separate area that would be governed by the international community.

This fiction never existed anywhere but on paper. It never existed because the Arabs rejected the partition proposal and started a war to prevent it from being realized. When they lost that war, Jerusalem west of the armistice line became Israel's, and Jerusalem east of the line came under Jordanian occupation and entered an extended period of disputed claims. So the U.S., while recognizing Israel within the armistice lines, chose a policy that held the status of Israel's capital hostage to a fiction that never had a chance of existing.

When Israel captured the eastern part of Jerusalem in 1967, during the Six-Day War, it moved to unite the Old City to the east with the residential city to the west, and in addition annexed dozens of Arab villages to create a massive municipal area that became what many Israeli politicians call "undivided" or "united" Jerusalem. This was indeed a controversial move, especially as it was followed by massive building of Jewish residential neighborhoods in that annexed area; this move continues to not be recognized by any country to this day. It is also controversial within Israel, where many Israelis continue to support the possibility that a future Palestinian state would have its capital in the eastern part of Jerusalem.

As the fiction of the "Corpus Separatum" faded from memory, Israel's annexation of the areas east of the 1967 line became the new reason for not recognizing any part of Jerusalem as Israel's capital. In this way, the U.S. has been punishing Israel twice: It has been denying any legitimate claims Israel had in Jerusalem east of the armistice line, including with respect to the Jewish holy sites in the Old City and the Jewish Quarter, and, until Trump's announcement, would not acknowledge that at the very least, west of that line, Jerusalem is legitimately Israel's capital.

Trump's declaration finally puts an end to this nonsensical policy. By dismissing the fiction of the "Corpus Separatum" at last, the U.S. can stop denying Israel, alone among the nations, a basic national sovereign right to establish its capital in undisputed territory.

Trump used only the ambiguous term "Jerusalem" in his speech, saying, "We are not taking a position on any final status issues, including the specific boundaries of the Israeli sovereignty in Jerusalem or the resolution of contested borders. Those questions are up to the parties involved." It would have been better if Trump had specified that the U.S. is only recognizing Israel's capital in Jerusalem west of 1967 line—in other words, that the U.S. is simply ending the illogical policy that holds the undisputed status of Jerusalem west of the armistice line hostage to the ongoing dispute over Jerusalem east of that line.

Nevertheless, if the U.S. continues to declare that Jerusalem's final borders should be negotiated (meaning that it leaves open the possibility of a Palestinian capital in the eastern part of Jerusalem), and if the U.S. refrains from describing Israel's capital as "united" or "undivided" Jerusalem, and if the U.S. continues to refrain from taking any steps that recognize Israel's annexation of the territories east of the 1967 line, and assuming that the new embassy will be located in Jerusalem west of that line—then Palestinian, Arab, and Muslim leaders who are not itching for violence should be able to legitimately say that Trump's declaration effectively changes nothing.

The Atlantic
December 6, 2017

Aligning Policy with Preference

Introduction

The repeated failure of Palestinian-Israeli negotiations to produce a peace agreement, and the growing sense that the two-state solution is in jeopardy, has prompted interest in the possibility that a more active international role might help enshrine the parameters of a two-state solution and salvage it as the prominent path to peace. This sentiment is particularly strong among some European countries, as evidenced by Sweden's October 2014 recognition of Palestine, France's (failed) December 2014 attempt to pass a draft UN Security Council resolution to that effect, the continuing efforts of France and New Zealand to reintroduce similar resolutions, the wave of resolutions in European parliaments calling upon their governments to recognize Palestine, and the EU's November 2015 publication of guidelines for labeling of products made in the Israeli settlements. Periodic speculation also suggests that certain conditions might lead the United States to support such an effort or, at the very least, not prevent other countries from doing so.

This pressure toward a greater international role in preserving the two-state solution could well intensify given the growing sense that—considering some of Israeli prime minister Binyamin Netanyahu's pronouncements and the stances of certain influential Israeli ministers and diplomatic appointees—the current Israeli government is no longer committed to this path. The pressure is compounded by the flare-up of violence across Israel, the West Bank, and Gaza, the rise of the boycott, divestment, and sanctions (BDS) movement, and Palestinian Authority (PA) president Mahmoud Abbas's persistent refusal to negotiate directly with Israel, while he calls on the international community to take greater action.

While the intellectual discussion of a "one-state solution" gains traction in certain circles, another trend involves the international community's apparent growing indifference to the conflict. This latter tendency was striking in U.S. president Barack Obama's omission of the conflict from his September 2015 UN speech. Even in light of various divergent trends, and the remaining wide gap between the Israeli and Palestinian sides, the two-state option continues to represent Western and international consensus as the preferred path to a just peace.

Proponents of a more active international role in advancing the two-state solution argue that it would explicitly enshrine parameters that the world already implicitly recognizes and, in doing so, ensure that any future negotiations would not start from scratch but rather build on previous progress. Enshrining such parameters, the thinking goes, would ultimately transform them into basic tenets of international relations, in the same way UN Security Council Resolution 242 turned the "land for peace" and direct negotiations formula into the foundation of the current international consensus on a two-state solution. Some even argue that a new Security Council resolution would serve to officially replace 242 as the basis for a new international consensus. It is further argued that while the parties are not expected to endorse these parameters, the very act of spelling out the necessary concessions would bring the conversation about permanent-status issues—dormant, and some would say even irrelevant, in both Israel and the PA in recent years—back to the forefront in both societies.

Given this environment, this paper aims to examine what policies might be pursued by the international community in general and Western governments in particular should they embark on a path that would align their current policies with their preference for a two-state solution to the Palestinian-Israeli conflict. The approach here is therefore intrinsically hypothetical and analytical, rather than prescriptive: that is, if various governments moved in the direction this paper explores, what tools would be at their disposal, what effects could be anticipated, and what policy combinations might be more or less constructive.

The analysis presented here does not make any assumptions about the motives, good or bad, wise or unwise, behind different official efforts along these lines. Moreover, the paper does not advocate or assume that all governments, or even just all European Union governments, would agree on all steps, nor that those steps would or should be codified in any internationally binding legal fashion, such as in a new Security Council resolution.

To examine what policies might be pursued, this study begins with three countries that have already taken active steps toward setting the terms for a two-state reality: Iceland, Sweden, and the Vatican.

Policymaking in the Absence of Direct Negotiations

On October 30, 2014, the Swedish government directly recognized the state of Palestine. This was the first time a major Western and European nation had taken such an action. (Iceland recognized Palestine in December 2011, and Malta and Cyprus recognized Palestine in 1988, when the two island nations were not yet EU members.) In declaring its decision, the Swedish government argued that its purpose was to contribute to a future where Israel and Palestine live "in peaceful coexistence with secure and recognized borders".

Sweden's decision took place amid a wave of votes in European parliaments calling on their governments to also directly recognize the state of Palestine. In June 2015, for its part, the Vatican formally recognized the state of Palestine by signing a diplomatic treaty with it. Archbishop Paul Gallagher, the Vatican's foreign secretary, declared, much like his Swedish counterpart, that the agreement could provide "stimulus to bringing a definitive end to the longstanding Palestinian-Israeli conflict." Given the possibility that additional Western governments could follow the lead of Iceland, Sweden, and the Vatican and respond to their respective parliaments' votes, it is imperative to carefully examine how, and whether, such actions could contribute to peace.

The decision by the Swedish government represented a fundamental break with Western policies toward the Palestinian-Israeli conflict and the two-state solution. Up until the moment of Sweden's declaration, Western countries—the United States, Canada, Australia, New Zealand, Britain, European states, the EU, and the

Vatican—broadly shared the same position regarding the promotion of peace between Israel and the Palestinians. This agreed upon position, which began with UN Security Council Resolution 242 but was later and more comprehensively expressed in the 2003 Roadmap peace initiative, has as its goal "a final and comprehensive permanent status agreement that ends the Israel-Palestinian conflict".

The Roadmap emphasizes that the goal should be reached "through a settlement negotiated between the parties." The agreement, once reached, would "fulfill the vision of two states, Israel and sovereign, independent, democratic, and viable Palestine." The agreement would also "end the occupation that began in 1967" and would "include an agreed, just, fair, and realistic solution to the refugee issue" as well as a *The underlying premise for aligning Western policies with preferences would be that a future resolution of the conflict by means of two states for two peoples would become easier to attain if existing policies assume this is already the reality.* "negotiated resolution on the status of Jerusalem that takes into account the political and religious concerns of both sides, and protects the religious interests of Jews, Christians, and Muslims worldwide." The agreement was likewise expected to lead to "a comprehensive Arab-Israeli peace" that includes "acceptance of full normal relations with Israel and security for all the states of the region."

Since the Roadmap was introduced, notable events, such as the unofficial Geneva Accord in 2003, Israel's disengagement from Gaza in 2005, and several rounds of unsuccessful talks between Israel and the Palestinians, while all failing to bring about peace, served to further shape and specify the manner in which Western countries view the desired outcome of a negotiated peace deal. For example, on borders, after Israel withdrew fully to the 1967 lines in Gaza, the issue of one-to-one land swaps became more firmly entrenched as a way to reconcile the existence of Israeli settlement blocs beyond the pre-1967 ceasefire lines in the West Bank with the Palestinian demand that these lines serve as the internationally recognized border.

Correspondingly, the idea that the future state of Palestine should be demilitarized and that a transitional Israel Defense Forces (IDF) presence should be stationed on the Jordan River was received favorably when suggested within a U.S. proposal for security arrangements following the establishment of a Palestinian state. The 2013–2014 round of talks led by U.S. secretary of state John Kerry also introduced the idea of allowing settlers to choose between relocating to Israel and staying where they were as loyal citizens of Palestine, although such an option has yet to become entrenched as a strong preference by Western countries.

On what is known as the Palestinian "right of return," or the demand of Arab refugees and displaced persons from the 1947–1949 war and their millions of descendants to forcefully return to Israel with full citizenship, more-concrete numbers were introduced in repeated rounds of negotiations and, although never agreed upon, became considered by Western countries as "fair and realistic." Further, whatever precise numbers were discussed, they were to be seen as reflecting "an end to all claims."

More than twenty years of negotiations, then, while failing to deliver peace or anything close to it, *have* yielded a broadly agreed upon set of preferences by all Western countries, allowing for differences in policy and tone. These preferences could be summarized as follows:

1. The establishment of an Arab Palestinian state side by side with the Jewish state of Israel—referred to in this paper as the question of *status*.

2. Recognized borders based on the 1967 lines with allowance for land swaps to adjust for the large settlement blocs, as well as a land connection between the West Bank and Gaza—referred to in this paper as the question of *borders*.

3. Jerusalem as the capital of both Israel and Palestine, generally meant with West Jerusalem as the capital of Israel, including residential Jewish neighborhoods in East Jerusalem in return for land swaps; residential Arab East Jerusalem as the capital of Palestine; and the Holy Basin, including the Old City, under special arrangements that secure religious freedom and access for all— referred to in this paper as the question of *Jerusalem*.

4. An "agreed, just, fair, and realistic solution to the refugee issue," which is generally taken to mean that the currently registered five million refugees— a figure including the several tens of thousands of the original displaced persons and refugees still alive and their millions of living descendants— would become citizens of the state of Palestine, with those residing in Jordan, Syria, and Lebanon offered options of either immigrating to the newly established state of Palestine, remaining as full and

equal citizens in their host countries, or becoming naturalized in third countries, including Israel, with Israel agreeing to absorb somewhere between several thousand and tens of thousands of displaced persons, refugees, and descendants over several years, and that this would represent an "end to all claims"—referred to in this paper as the question of *displaced persons, refugees, and their descendants.*

These four main questions have constituted the core of Palestinian-Israeli talks over the past two decades. Moreover, until Iceland, Sweden, and the Vatican directly recognized Palestine as a state, *all* Western countries shared the Roadmap position that "a final and comprehensive" deal should be "negotiated between the parties" and that the solution is to be "agreed."

The preference for a negotiated agreement meant that despite substantial differences in tone, Western countries abstained from taking steps that would circumvent negotiations. Although Western countries had clear preferences on the desired outcome, they did not take major steps to reflect those preferences. In many cases, this meant that Western countries' official policies on the four major issues were not necessarily aligned with their preferences. For example, even if a particular Western country thought a Palestinian state desirable, it did not recognize Palestine, arguing that such a state should emerge as the outcome of a negotiated peace agreement. is meant that up until the decisions by Iceland, Sweden, and the Vatican, Western countries held back from establishing "facts on the ground" that would "prejudice" the outcome of the negotiations in one direction or another.

Sweden's decision, although preceded by Iceland's

in December 2011, represented a dramatic break from traditional Western policies. While Sweden continues to call on the sides to negotiate an agreement and declared that it will "support renewed negotiations on a final status settlement," the country's action reflected a frustration that "peace talks have again stalled." Indeed, Sweden's action came at a point when more and more countries had concluded that the preference for process—negotiations—had failed to lead to the preferred outcome—a comprehensive permanent-status agreement that ends the conflict. Iceland, Sweden, and the Vatican have turned the Western position on its head: *rather than support negotiations that lead to a certain outcome that would support peace, they supported a certain outcome in the hopes that it would lead to negotiations that would bring about peace.*

It remains to be seen to what extent and in which manner Western governments will seek to follow Iceland, Sweden, and the Vatican and "prejudice" the outcome in a way that aligns their policies with their stated preferences. In the past, the preference of Western countries for negotiations has led them to maintain that they do not wish to prejudice the final outcome by promoting policies that favor one side's position over the other. Yet Western governments, increasingly frustrated by the continuing failure of negotiations to achieve a resolution, might choose to reverse this equation and, in effect, prejudice a desired outcome to the conflict by more closely aligning their policies with their preferences. Expressing such frustration, France's foreign minister, Laurent Fabius, declared during the French parliament's discussion on voting for Palestinian recognition that "in view of the current deadlock, we think it's legitimate to opt for an approach enabling us to give negotiation a genuine and perhaps a final chance...Support—some will say pressure—is required from the international community to help both sides make the final, essential gesture and take the ultimate step that will lead to peace. That's what the French government is focusing on right now."

Robert Serry, the former UN special coordinator for the Middle East peace process, told the Security Council that European votes on Palestinian recognition are "significant developments that serve to highlight growing impatience at the continued lack of real progress in achieving a two-state solution...governments are under increased public pressure to promote an end to the conflict once and for all." Thus, Western countries appear increasingly to share Abbas's claim in his 2015 UN General Assembly speech that "it is no longer useful to waste time in negotiations for the sake of negotiations; what is required is to mobilize international efforts to oversee an end to the occupation in line with the resolutions of international legitimacy."

Beyond the broadly shared frustration, Sweden justified "breaking rank" with the traditional Western position of not taking steps to circumvent negotiations by suggesting its own analysis for the failure of negotiations. The essence of Sweden's argument is that recognition of Palestine would "facilitate an agreement by making the parties in these negotiations less unequal." The underlying premise then is that negotiations have failed, at least in part, because Israel and Palestine are "unequal" and that recognizing the state of Palestine would make the Palestinians less unequal, and thereby contribute to the attainment of peace. Fundamentally, Sweden is arguing that recognizing Palestine *prior* to negotiations, rather than as the direct *outcome* of them, would help achieve peace. This premise could be debated, accepted, or rejected, but what remains in effect is that Sweden's action, and those of Iceland and the Vatican, represents an instance of establishing "facts on the ground" and *prejudicing a certain outcome, regardless of negotiations or agreements.*

If more Western governments chose to align their policies with their preference for peace by means of "two states for two peoples," they might pursue a range of policies that would approximate such a reality on the ground, even if no such agreement has been made. The premise of such policies would be that of a "self-fulfilling prophecy." That is, the underlying premise for aligning Western policies with preferences would be that *a future resolution of the conflict by means of two states for two peoples would become easier to attain if existing policies assume this is already the reality.*

Two questions thereby require further analysis:

1. What other possible policy steps might Western countries seek if they are on the path to aligning their policies with their preferences?
2. Are such steps more or less likely to bring about peace?

To answer the first question, this paper will explore the policy tools that Western countries have at their disposal should they choose to align their policies with their stated preferences to prejudice certain outcomes. The paper will begin by analyzing existing gaps between the stated preferences for outcomes and current policies. It will then look at the manner in which certain policies could close these gaps and the challenges associated with implementing those policies.

This paper neither explores nor recommends means of

pressuring Israel and the Palestinians to adopt certain policies. It restricts itself to policies that are *entirely within the decisionmaking power and control of Western countries* and that enable them to align their policies with their preferences for a desired outcome. These are policies Western countries can pursue without requiring the Palestinian or Israeli side to respond to, accept, or reject their policy changes. The paper also restricts itself to "hard currency" concrete diplomatic and economic policies and positions that go beyond declarations and speeches.

Regarding the second question—whether such steps would contribute to peace—the paper will explore the possible implications of such actions by Western countries, and especially the implications of picking and choosing certain elements of a final-status agreement rather than addressing them all as a grand package. Should more countries take measures to align their policies with their preferences, such a path would have serious ramifications for the conflict and for the region. Even if some of the measures reviewed here would not be taken up by Western governments fully and immediately, this project is intended to consider the general ramifications of such measures and the consequences regarding any future agreement.

The West: Current Policies

While the preferences of Western countries have been expressed in numerous formats and forums, as well as in joint declarations such as the Roadmap, official policies generally remain attached to the last "solid" internationally agreed upon point of reference, which in some cases means going as far back as the UN partition proposal of 1947. As a result, wide gaps have opened between policies based on what can be justified de jure and the preferences de facto, resulting in sometimes convoluted policy positions.

STATUS

On the matter of status, the official position of all Western countries, except for Iceland, Sweden, and the Vatican (and Cyprus and Malta before joining the EU), is that an independent Arab state of Palestine *does not exist* and therefore should not be recognized as such. However, the clear preference of all Western countries is that such a state *should exist*. As a result, numerous policies have been taken to reflect that preference, including providing the Palestinians with as many trappings of a state as possible but without crossing the line to officially recognizing a state. For many years, especially since 1993, this has meant, for example, treating the PA as a state for purposes of official visits and viewing its diplomats abroad as ambassadors.

In recent years, this policy of recognizing the trappings of a state of Palestine without recognizing the state of Palestine itself was advanced even further when, on November 29, 2012, 138 countries voted in the UN General Assembly for recognizing Palestine as a nonmember observer state, with 9 voting against and 41 abstaining. The Western vote was split, with 19 countries voting in favor (Austria, Belgium, Cyprus, Denmark, Finland, France, Greece, Iceland, Ireland, Italy, Liechtenstein, Luxembourg, Malta, New Zealand, Norway, Portugal, Spain, Sweden, and Switzerland); 3 voting against (the United States, Canada, and the Czech Republic); and 14 abstaining (Australia, Bulgaria, Croatia, Estonia, Germany, Hungary, Latvia, Lithuania, the Netherlands, Poland, Romania, Slovakia, Slovenia, and Britain) (see appendix 7 for the UN press release).

In a September 2015 follow-up, the General Assembly voted to raise the flags of nonmember observer states, effectively enabling the Palestinian flag to fly alongside those of UN member states. The vote passed with the support of 119 countries, with 8 voting against and 45 abstaining. The Western results were marked by several votes in favor from the 2012 measure now abstaining (Austria, Cyprus, Denmark, Finland, Greece, Liechtenstein, Portugal, Switzerland, and Norway), along with the Czech Republic, a 2012 "no" vote. Countries remaining in the yes column were Belgium, France, Iceland, Ireland, Italy, Luxembourg, Malta, New Zealand, Spain, and Sweden. Only two 2012 abstentions, Poland and Slovenia, switched to yes votes. As a whole, the Western tally remained split, with Australia, Canada, and the United States voting against.

While these votes represent symbolic steps in the process of aligning Western policies with preferences on the status issue, they also exposed the gaps between Western countries regarding their actual policies and their differing perceptions as to the outcomes their diplomatic tactics would yield: countries that voted against the 2012 and 2015 resolutions or abstained, such as the United States, Australia, and Germany, argued that the vote "placed further obstacles in the path to peace" (United States) and might "make a negotiated solution more difficult" (Australia) and "lead to further hardening of positions" (Germany).

Some countries that voted for the 2012 resolution, such as Switzerland, expressed hope for precisely the opposite outcome: that the vote would "unblock the current stalemate." Also, while Canada voted against both resolutions because it "undermined the core foundations of the decades-long commitment by the international community" (i.e., to the process of negotiations), Spain voted in favor both times because the vote was "an expression of the international community's firm and irreversible commitment to peace" (i.e., to this outcome).

Among the European countries that voted in favor of the 2012 resolution, varying justifications were given. Norway, for example, argued that Palestine was already "involved in many institutions as a functioning state" and that recognition was a natural outcome, while Finland described its vote in favor as "showing support to the moderate forces that were committed to the peace process."

The one point of consensus among the Western countries voting in favor both in 2012 and in 2015 was that the vote "endowed the Palestinians with obligations" (Switzerland). Many diplomats of the countries voting in favor of nonmember observer status have taken pains to emphasize that the vote should lead to a return to direct negotiations to fully resolve the conflict. It was understood that the vote was not meant to grant full sovereignty to the Palestinians, although it was a step in that direction. Diplomats have stated that voting for a state of Palestine in the UN is not the same as directly and unilaterally recognizing an independent state of Palestine, although many readily admit that this is a very fine line—but a line they insist on defending.

Iceland, Sweden, and the Vatican are the first Western countries to cross the fine line and fully align their policies with their preference regarding the status of the state of Palestine. When, on October 30, 2014, Sweden officially and directly recognized Palestine as a state already in existence, it argued that "the international law criteria for the recognition of the State of Palestine have been satisfied." According to the government of Sweden, this means "there is a territory, albeit with non-defined borders. There is also a population. And there is a government with the capacity for internal and external control."

In the months following the 2012 UN vote, the parliaments of Ireland, Spain, France, Luxembourg, Portugal, and Britain passed nonbinding resolutions calling on their governments to directly recognize the state of Palestine. More parliaments are considering such votes, meaning that more countries might follow Iceland, Sweden, and the Vatican. If this were to happen, additional countries would have aligned their preference with their policies, recognizing the state of Palestine and thereby contending that it already exists.

BORDERS

The official policy of all Western governments is that the cease fire agreement lines of 1967 represent the limit to the internationally accepted area under Israeli sovereignty and that all territory beyond that, even if annexed by Israel, is not legally Israel's. Since, for most Western countries, an official state of Palestine does not exist and is not recognized—and even for those governments that do recognize the state of Palestine—the 1967 lines are not considered official and internationally recognized borders between the state of Israel and the state of Palestine. The official Western position recognizes the state of Israel to the west of the 1967 lines and the not-yet-state of Palestine to the east and south of these lines (the West Bank and Gaza). Sweden has argued that Palestine has a "nondefined border" but has indicated that this border is, or should be, the 1967 lines by referring in its recognition statement to Palestine as existing in the West Bank and Gaza.

With respect to Gaza, Israel has, in effect, accepted the 1967 lines by fully withdrawing to these lines in 2005. This means that on the question of Gaza, there is no longer a territorial dispute between Israel and the Palestinians. Even though Israel controls Gaza's airspace and enforces a security blockade, these actions are declared as serving security purposes and Israel no longer makes a territorial claim on Gaza.

Whereas the question of settlements and Israeli territorial claims in Gaza is now moot, the West Bank is still very much in dispute, especially regarding the Jewish settlements. On this issue, no substantial policy difference exists among Western countries, even if they differ in tone. The West Bank settlements, regardless of where they are located, are considered by all Western governments to be illegal, or "in violation of the Fourth Geneva Convention" (Canada), or "contrary to international law" (U.S. Department of State). This means that all varieties of settlements are considered by Western governments to be equally illegal, including Jewish neighborhoods of East Jerusalem, the Jewish communities of Gush Etzion that were rebuilt on Jewish agricultural towns destroyed by Arab League forces in the 1948 war, and settlements on private Palestinian territory.

It is worth noting that, in January 2014, the Australian foreign minister made a comment that questioned this position and called on the international community to refrain from calling settlements illegal under international law, but it is not clear whether this is official Australian policy. While it is true that strong legal and historical arguments can be made that Israeli settlement activity in the West Bank territories is not illegal, these arguments have been marginalized and the reigning consensus is that the settlements are not legal.

As such, all Western countries are opposed to further expansion of settlements and make their displeasure at any such activity well known. While the language differs, the tone is negative across the board. For example, French president Francois Hollande stated that he "demands the entire and definitive halt to the settlement activity." The German government has been "urging an end to the construction," with the British adopting a similar tone. Some countries, such as Spain, are no less negative but use passive rather than active language to express their regret and condemnation.

Beyond the language and the clear expressions against settlements in general and settlement expansion in particular, European countries have in recent years taken punitive action to reinforce their view of the settlements as illegal. Such steps have included the banning of imports of dairy, eggs, and poultry from agricultural settlements in the West Bank; the September 2015 adoption by the European Parliament of a resolution, " The EU's Role in the Middle East Peace Process," that "welcomed" the EU's commitment to "differentiation" between Israel and the "occupied Palestinian Territory"; and the November 2015 release by the European Commission of the "Interpretative Notice on Indication of Origin of Goods from the Territories Occupied by Israel since 1967." The "Interpretative Notice" emphasized that "the aim is to ensure the respect of Union positions and commitments in conformity with international law on the non-recognition by the Union of Israel's sovereignty over the territories occupied by Israel since June 1967."

Even though Western governments consider the settlements illegal, some, especially the United States, Canada, and Australia, have acknowledged that any future peace agreement would have to consider the "facts on the ground" regarding the large settlement blocs, most of which are adjacent to the 1967 line. They believe that the manner in which this will happen should be negotiated and agreed upon between the sides. This was most prominently acknowledged by President George W. Bush in his April 14, 2004, letter to Prime Minister Ariel Sharon, which said that "in light of new realities on the ground, including already existing major Israeli population centers, it is unrealistic to expect that the outcome of final status negotiations will be a full and complete return to the armistice lines of 1949, and all previous efforts to negotiate a two-state solution have reached the same conclusion. It is realistic to expect that any final status agreement will only be achieved on the basis of mutually agreed changes that reflect these realities."

Western governments broadly accept that nearly all the West Bank and Gaza should belong to the future state of Palestine and that the areas where the large settlement blocs lie would belong to Israel, in exchange for land elsewhere (land swaps), so that, in effect, the state of Palestine would control precisely the same *amount of area* that comprises the West Bank and Gaza, if not *precisely the same area*. While there is no agreement as to which settlement blocs should be assumed "forgone" for Israel and to the precise size of the land swaps, estimates, based on previous rounds of negotiations, range from 2 to 9 percent of the West Bank's land area.

Even the Arab League expressed its support for the

notion of land swaps when in April 2013 a delegation of its foreign ministers and ambassadors accepted the principle of "comparable" and "minor" land swaps as part of a permanent-status agreement. Speaking on behalf of the Arab League, Sheikh Hamad bin Jassim al-Thani, Qatar's prime minister and foreign minister, explained to journalists that the League supports Israel and the Palestinians swapping territory rather than conforming to the 1967 borders.

No Western government currently pursues a policy that fully acknowledges the possibility of land swaps. In this sense, Western policy is "over- shooting" by taking action that strictly insists on the 1967 lines. For example, when the EU pursues policies that differentiate between the West Bank and Israel in its economic agreements, it does not include the settlement blocs as part of Israel and makes no allowance for the possibility of land swaps. In fact, the European countries and the EU seem to be moving toward intensifying measures that differentiate between "legal Israel" and "illegal Israel" along the 1967 lines, without any consideration for the possibility of land swaps. Similarly, while the United States acknowledges, in principle, that not all settlements are alike and some will permanently belong to Israel, it engages in "overshooting" by condemning Israel equally for all settlement building, regardless of location.

JERUSALEM

The official position of all Western governments is that Jerusalem is *not* the capital of the state of Israel. In addition, all Western countries continue to treat, in principle, the whole of Jerusalem as belonging to no one. Western countries continue to formally adhere to the position put forward in the 1947 UN partition proposal of Jerusalem as a *corpus separatum* deserving separate international status. For example, the U.S. Department of State does not register American nationals born in Jerusalem as having been born in Israel. However, the expressed preference of all Western governments is for Jerusalem to serve as the capital of *both* the state of Israel and the future state of Palestine, with West Jerusalem and some Jewish neighborhoods of East Jerusalem to be part of Israel, and the Arab neighborhoods of East Jerusalem to be the capital of Palestine—a preference most notably put forth in the Clinton Parameters following the 2000 Camp David negotiations. Regarding the one-square-kilometer area of the Holy Basin, which includes Jerusalem's Old City and some adjacent sites, the preference is for some form of special status and governance that would ensure freedom of religious practice and access for all. This preference is repeatedly reiterated when religious tensions and questions of access to holy sites in the Basin lead to are-ups of violence.

Some European declarations treat East Jerusalem as the future capital of Palestine without making distinctions—neither between Jewish and Arab neighborhoods nor between the Holy Basin and residential areas. In addition, many countries have consulates in East Jerusalem that form part of the "Consular Corps of the Corpus Separatum," with their members effectively serving as ambassadors to Palestine. Sweden itself has announced that it will not open an embassy in Ramallah and that its bilateral diplomatic relations with the recognized state of Palestine "can be managed by the consulate in Jerusalem, which is a satisfactory solution for us."

The official policy of Western governments rests on the 1947 UN proposal for Jerusalem as a *corpus separatum*, but the preferences are more directly related to the 1967 lines, distinguishing between an Israeli West Jerusalem and a Palestinian East Jerusalem. This creates a situation whereby East Jerusalem is considered under illegal occupation and sometimes referred to as "occupied Palestinian territory" or "occupied East Jerusalem" but residential West Jerusalem, which no country effectively disputes as belonging to Israel, is not considered a legitimate location for Israel's capital. *Israel is judged by 1947, but the Palestinians are judged by 1967.* The case of Sweden makes this distinction most glaring: Sweden now has, in effect, an official embassy to Palestine located in East Jerusalem even as it continues to refuse to move its official embassy in Israel from Tel Aviv to West Jerusalem. is means the de jure status of West Jerusalem as belonging to Israel and serving as its capital is held hostage de facto until the situation of East Jerusalem is resolved.

DISPLACED PERSONS, REFUGEES, AND THEIR DESCENDANTS

The official policy of all Western governments is to treat the question of Palestinian displaced persons and refugees from the 1947–1949 war and their millions of descendants as a final-status issue that the governments do not want to prejudice. On the specific issue of "right of return," most Western governments do not hold an official policy and do not weigh in on the purported legality of such a right, reiterating a call to resolve the issue between the parties in an agreed, just, and realistic manner.

The solution that all Western governments consider

"just and realistic" includes the following stated preferences:

- Palestinian displaced persons, refugees, and their descendants will have the right to live in and become citizens of the state of Palestine. This will effectively mean that their right is to self-determination in a state of their own, where they can then legislate a law of return. Such a law would then allow Palestinians around the world to exercise their "right of return" to the newly established state of Palestine, but that "right" would not be for any other place, country, or territory.

- The countries today home to the largest populations of refugees and displaced persons and descendants—Jordan, Lebanon, and Syria, although many fewer in Syria as a result of the civil war—would be encouraged to absorb and fully integrate as many of the descendants as wish to live there.

- Third countries, including Israel, would also each take a share of the displaced persons, refugees, and their descendants, with numbers for Israel generally quoted in the several thousands, with the clear stipulation that any such numbers would be finite and represent an "end to all claims."

- Compensation would be provided to displaced persons, refugees, and their descendants, to which the state of Israel, along with Western and Arab countries, would contribute. In this context, the possibility has been raised of parallel Arab compensation for descendants of

Jews expelled from Arab countries in revenge for the establishment of the state of Israel, but this is yet to become broadly accepted.

In direct contradiction to this set of preferences, all Western governments are substantial contributors to the UN Relief and Works Agency for Palestine Refugees in the Near East, for a total of more than $1 billion a year. While UNRWA serves important social and welfare functions, such as the provision of health care, assistance, and education to descendants of Palestinian displaced persons and refugees, it also engages in political practices, such as automatically granting all descendants of the original displaced persons and refugees the status of refugees themselves—regardless of their actual situation. This has led to the registration of nearly five million descendants, the majority of whom are either Jordanian citizens or citizens of the PA residing in the Gaza Strip or West Bank. The organization also teaches the "right of return" in schools, telling the descendants of the originally displaced persons and refugees that they have the individual and uncontestable right to forcefully return to areas that are part of the state of Israel. In their support for UNRWA, Western governments, even if unintentionally, are in effect condoning UNRWA's political practices—practices that depart sharply both from Western official positions and preferences.

In conversations, diplomats have rejected the notion that supporting UNRWA financially means support for a literal implementation of the "right of return" and have tended to downplay the seriousness with which the Palestinians treat this right. However, a groundbreaking October 2014 report by the International Crisis Group underscores the extent to which Western diplomats underestimate the importance that the Palestinians attach to this demand. It also underscores the "almost supernatural significance" Palestinians attribute to UNRWA as embodying international support for their demand for a "return to Palestine." Unique in understanding and supporting UNRWA's political function is Norway, which officially states that it views UNRWA as "a guarantor that the rights of Palestine refugees, including the right to return, are not forgotten."

The case of Sweden is again particularly instructive. Sweden is one of the largest single-state donors to UNRWA and, therefore, effectively supports UNRWA's practice of registering descendants of displaced persons born and living in the West Bank and Gaza as refugees from Palestine. Since Sweden has recognized the state of Palestine and argues that it exists and that the territories of the West Bank and Gaza are Palestine, it is difficult to explain how it can continue to support registering those living and born *in* Palestine—and never displaced from it—as refugees *from* Palestine. This can only be explained if Sweden accepts that Palestine is not limited to the West Bank and Gaza and will supersede what is today the state of Israel. is means that Swedish recognition of Palestine, as long as it continues to be paired with support for UNRWA's practice of registering those born and living *in* Palestine as refugees *from* Palestine, is incompatible with the promotion of peace by means of two states for two peoples.

SUMMARY

This review of the alignment of policies with preferences of Western countries demonstrates that, except in the case of Iceland, Sweden, and the

Vatican on the question of status, *in no major policy area are the policies of Western countries fully aligned with their preferences, and in most cases they are misaligned or even contradictory to their stated preferences.*

In light of this assessment, should more countries seek to take steps that promote a certain outcome rather than wait for this outcome to be negotiated between the parties, several policy options could emerge by closing the gaps between their stated preferences and their existing policies. The purpose of the following section is to explore which policy tools are available to Western countries on this path, and highlight diplomatic and political challenges that need to be factored in if such a path is followed.

If Policies Aligned with Preferences
In contrast to the launch of permanent-status negotiations in 2000, today the international community and the parties themselves have a better understanding of both the substance of the permanent-status issues and the realistic options associated with each, should a peacemaking context emerge. This, however, does not amount to a consensus on the contours—let alone the details—of a preferred final peace deal. If Western countries sought to align their policies with their preferences, they would have to delve into details and consider the specifics of various options to craft coherent policies.

STATUS
The issue of status—that is, the recognition of the state of Palestine—is the one for which Western countries are most likely to seek to align their policies with their preferences, given that it requires the least consideration of

details and is relatively straightforward to implement. Such implementation can be done through any of three major policy tools—listed here in decreasing order of likelihood of use:

1. Supporting Palestine in various UN bodies as the PA continues on the path of seeking to upgrade its status in the UN and its associated bodies.
2. Fully and bilaterally recognizing an already existing state of Palestine, as Iceland, Sweden, and the Vatican have done and as several European parliaments have voted requesting their governments to do.
3. Voting for a UN Security Council resolution that recognizes the state of Palestine and admits it into the UN as a full member state.

With respect to the policy tool of supporting Palestine in international bodies, to date the Palestinians have indicated their intention to join at least sixty UN bodies and treaties, and have so far submitted requests to join at least fifteen. While the legal status and procedures for joining each UN body and treaty are different, Western countries would likely be asked to vote for admitting Palestine on several occasions and might increasingly do so to emphasize their preference for the existence of a state of Palestine. For example, the director of the UN Educational, Scientific, and Cultural Organization (UNESCO) allowed the Palestinian request for membership to come to a vote in October 2011. The state of Palestine was admitted as a full member, with 107 voting in favor, 14 against, and 52 abstaining. In January 2015, the state of Palestine moved to join the International Criminal Court (ICC) at the Hague and in April was admitted as the 123rd member, based on its upgraded status as a result of the 2012 UN vote.

The policy tool of recognizing Palestine in international bodies is likely to be used by many Western countries because even with numerous and repeated UN votes for a state of Palestine, and Palestinian admittance to the ICC, this policy tool remains within the current Western policy of acknowledging the trappings of a state of Palestine without officially recognizing the state itself. The only country that faces challenges in implementing this policy is the United States, which currently has legislation mandating a complete cutoff of financing to any UN agency that accepts the Palestinians as a full member. This policy has led the United States to lose its UNESCO voting rights, which are tied to payment of dues.

On the second policy tool, direct recognition of Palestine: with more governments declaring that they are considering this tool, it might also become more widespread, especially if the continuing sense is that the negotiations remain stalled. While this represents a "breaking of ranks" with the traditional consensus of Western policies, it does bring Western policies into full alignment with preferences. In fact, it could eventually become the new consensus, with countries adopting the Swedish argument that the step promotes rather than hinders peace.

On the third policy tool, a UN Security Council resolution: despite the failure thus far to secure Security Council support for an official vote on a proposal that would recognize the state of Palestine and set a deadline for "ending the Israeli occupation of Palestine," the Palestinians are expected to renew this effort with the support of Security Council members France and New

Zealand. Even with a Security Council makeup deemed more supportive of votes relating to Palestine, for such a vote to pass, the veto-wielding Western countries, and especially the United States, would have to either support the resolution or abstain from vetoing it.

In this context, it is worth noting that increasing numbers of Israeli public figures are supporting recognition of Palestinian statehood. In October 2014, more than three hundred Israeli public figures signed a letter to British MPs encouraging them to vote in their parliament in support of recognizing Palestine. The letter, initiated by former director-general of the Israeli Foreign Ministry Alon Liel, was signed by six winners of the prestigious Israel Prize, former Israeli ministers and Knesset members, and former Israeli attorney general and Supreme Court justice Michael Ben-Yair.

In an August 2015 *New York Times* op-ed, Hilik Bar, a Knesset member who is secretary-general of the Labor Party, argued that Israel should recognize a Palestinian state at the UN because "the dispute should no longer be about whether there will be two states, but about the details of an agreement." Such statements by Israeli public figures provide positive reinforcement to Western states and diplomats who believe recognizing a Palestinian state would be beneficial to Israel and the cause of peace.

BORDERS

Should Western governments align their policies with their preferences on borders to avoid the current "overshooting," they would need to make preliminary judgments on which settlement blocs they would consider as properly belonging to Israel. Currently, no international consensus exists about what constitutes a "bloc" and which of the blocs would be part of Israel in a final peace deal. But if Western governments sought to employ a coherent and aligned policy on this issue, they would have to put forth a map and chart a proposed border. In attempting to do so, Western governments would probably find reaching a consensus difficult, and would likely accept only the most minimal assessment of 2 to 4 percent of the West Bank land area for the settlement blocs.

Once Western governments have cleared the hurdle of putting forth a proposed map and borders, their policies could then be fine-tuned and rebalanced to distinguish between the state of Israel—including the settlement blocs—and the state of Palestine. This would mean that any building within the recognized borders of Israel would no longer be considered illegal and would not lead to any negative consequences. With respect to Jewish settlements within Palestine, Western governments could condition export of products from Jewish communities in areas designated within the state of Palestine on the Palestinian government's agreement. This policy might be expanded to people as well, with Israeli citizens living in areas designated for Palestine being requested to obtain Palestinian passports for travel to Western countries, treating them in effect as citizens of Palestine.

Depending on Israel's actions—such as withdrawals from the areas designated as Palestine—Western countries might choose not only to recognize the state of Palestine within clear borders but also to designate some parts of Palestine as fully free, partly free, or under occupation of a foreign power, so as to indicate that recognition of Palestine as a state does not automatically imply that it is fully sovereign and free of foreign military occupation.

Even if a more coherent and aligned policy would require putting forth a map and delineating a border, the far greater likelihood is that Western countries would find the effort too difficult and continue on the current path of treating all settlements beyond the 1967 line equally. This is a less coherent policy in that it does not account for the established possibility of land swaps as a means toward incorporating the settlement blocs into Israel. This means correspondingly that this policy departs substantially from what a final-status agreement would look like and is "overly strict." However, considerations of ease of implementation seem at this juncture to overrule coherence.

JERUSALEM

Should Western governments decide to align their policies with preferences on the issue of Jerusalem, they would leave behind the 1947 partition proposal and pursue policies based on the 1967 lines. This means that policies would enshrine the international consensus that the capitals of both states would be in Jerusalem. Indeed, the more Western countries insist on the 1967 lines in differentiating Israel from the West Bank, the more it becomes nonsensical to continue treating West Jerusalem according to the 1947 proposal.

This means that in practice, West Jerusalem would be universally recognized and accepted not only as belonging to Israel but also as serving as the capital of the state of Israel. All countries would move their embassies to West Jerusalem to demonstrate this preference. In parallel, Western governments would recognize residential Arab East Jerusalem as the capital of the state of Palestine, with embassies moved there or existing consulates upgraded to fulfill the role. In addition, taking the Clinton Parameters as a guide, the Jewish neighborhoods of East Jerusalem would be accepted as belonging to Israel—just like the settlement blocs—with designated swaps.

With respect to Jerusalem's core, in the absence of a negotiated agreement that would determine questions of sovereignty or lack thereof over the Holy Basin, policies would emphasize securing freedom of religious observance and access to all and maintaining the web of arrangements of the status quo. The concept of the *corpus separatum* could then remain but be limited to the Holy Basin.

DISPLACED PERSONS, REFUGEES, AND THEIR DESCENDANTS

Should Western governments decide to align their policies with their preferences regarding the issue of the Palestinian refugees and their descendants, they could implement several policies that would address UNRWA's political practices. As voluntary donors to UNRWA, Western governments have substantial leeway in shaping the agency's practices. Any notion that Western governments cannot affect UNRWA's policies because its mandate is the charge of the General Assembly, where they are outnumbered, ignores the broad and open-to-interpretation terms of the General Assembly mandate, as well as the dependency of UNRWA, as an organization not budgeted by the UN, on the funding of Western donor countries.

If Western governments recognized a state of Palestine in the West Bank and Gaza, or even if they merely continued to pursue policies that differentiate between Israel and the West Bank and Gaza, any continued support for UNRWA's current policies would mean that

Western countries support the idea that those living *in* Palestine are also refugees *from* Palestine. This would not only make no sense, it would also send a devastating message regarding the idea of a peace based on the solution of two states for two peoples. It would mean the idea of a "Greater Palestine" to one day supersede Israel enjoys the support of Western countries and that a state of Palestine in the West Bank and Gaza does not represent the limits and final demands of the Palestinian people.

Even if the state of Palestine were recognized as existing under foreign occupation, that in itself would not justify registering people living in those areas as refugees, as they would still be living in their own state with the vast majority of them, being descendants, never having been displaced from their homes. To promote a coherent policy aligned with their preference for a solution based on two states for two peoples, Western governments could then insist, in their role as voluntary UNRWA donors, that UNRWA no longer register anyone living *in* Palestine as a refugee *from* Palestine.

With respect to the refugees and descendants living in Jordan, Lebanon, and Syria, Western countries could recognize the granting of Palestinian citizenship for all purposes, including travel. This means that the refugees and their descendants would become citizens of Palestine residing in Jordan, Syria, and Lebanon, enabling the latter three countries to preserve their existing demographic interests pending a final peace agreement.

Western governments could then pursue policies intended to enable those Palestinian citizens to enter the state of Palestine, be integrated into their host countries, or be naturalized in a third country, including Israel. UNRWA would enter a gradual process of effective dissolution, with hospital, education, and welfare operations in the West Bank and Gaza transferred to the state of Palestine and operations in Jordan, Syria, and Lebanon restricted to social services with the goal of transferring these operations to the host countries.

To the extent that the citizens living outside the recognized state of Palestine are prevented from entering the state, they could be recognized as refugees from the state of Palestine in the West Bank and Gaza with no claims whatsoever to being refugees from any areas within the state of Israel. The issue of compensation could, and should, be pursued separately.

A misperception prevails that ending refugee status, including for descendants, would forfeit their right to compensation for lost property. *There is absolutely no connection between refugee status and the right to compensation.* The descendants of the Arab refugees from the 1947–1949 war have the right to compensation for property that belonged to their ancestors and was lost due to the war. The fact that the descendants of the Arab refugees are granted "hereditary refugee" status has no bearing on the right to compensation. If Western governments want to send a clear message that ending registered refugee status will not threaten the right to compensation, they could support projects intended to map and assess the proper compensation due to all descendants. In addition, some of the funds currently going to UNRWA might be redirected to the purpose of compensation.

SUMMARY

In summary, if Western governments were to pursue policies more closely aligned with their stated preferences for a two-state outcome, they would have at their disposal several major policy tools—from recognizing a state of Palestine to moving their embassy to West Jerusalem to recognizing currently registered refugees as citizens of Palestine. *These tools are entirely within Western countries' control and do not require their rejection or acceptance by Israel or the Palestinians.*

Before looking into the implications of such potential policy changes, one note must be made regarding the military occupation of the West Bank and the control Israel exerts over three of Gaza's four borders. While no international support exists for Israel's continued military occupation of the West Bank or its partial control of Gaza's borders, there is broad support for Israel's security concerns regarding the Palestinian use of Gaza and the West Bank as launching pads for attacks against Israel. As such, modest support can be found among Western countries for demilitarizing the Palestinian state and allowing a transitional Israeli military presence on the Jordan River. Western governments could make clear that even if they recognize Palestine, they still consider it, or parts of it, under military occupation and that any future agreement would have to be based on a demilitarized Palestinian state.

On both of these elements, ending Israel's military occupation and addressing Israel's security concerns, Western governments lack policy options that can be enacted without the consent and agreement of Israelis and Palestinians. This paper, as noted, only examines policies under the complete control of Western powers. While the tools discussed here are diplomatically powerful, they cannot remove even one soldier from the West Bank or remove a single rocket from Gaza or disarm a West Bank attacker. Ultimately, even if Western governments fully align their policies with their states' preferences, the military situation on the ground will remain the one issue within the full control of the two sides and will have to be negotiated directly between them to achieve a true and durable peace.

Implications of Such Policy Alignment

Should Western governments choose to more fully align their policies with their preferences for a two-state outcome, this would represent a substantial change to the diplomatic environment in which the actors make their decisions. The extent of the change and the implications depend heavily on whether Western countries will seek to form a consensus prior to implementing the new policies and whether they would employ a "package" or a "pick-and-choose" approach in aligning their policies with their respective preferences. Iceland, Sweden, and the Vatican have already demonstrated one path by both breaking with consensus and employing a pick-and-choose approach, picking and choosing to address only the status of the Palestinian state among the various policy options.

Through their actions, the governments of Sweden, Iceland, and the Vatican have signaled that they do not think there is a need for consensus. They have demonstrated that individual countries, or blocs of countries, could adopt their own sets of positions and begin realigning their policies accordingly. The benefit of this approach is that it is easy to implement, requiring no prior coordination with fellow Western countries. It likewise enables a country such as Sweden to position itself as a policy leader but avoid delving into the details of more complex issues such as borders, Jerusalem, and those of displaced persons, refugees, and descendants. However, this approach carries its own risks since it could create further confusion—and possibly even contradiction—in the international community. Rather than enshrining agreed parameters, the approach could highlight the lack of consensus.

IS CONSENSUS NECESSARY?

The breadth of Western support for a given set of revised parameters on the core issues in the Palestinian-Israeli conflict will influence the margin of maneuverability for Israel and the Palestinians when formulating their responses. Opposing such parameters would be easier for the parties if they perceive them as representing the views of only few and peripheral countries.

In particular, the parties will be looking at whether such parameters are supported by their respective traditional allies. The more such allies are seen as firmly backing these ideas, the harder it would be for the parties to dismiss them. It is likely then that Palestinians and Israelis would mobilize their supporters to create and exploit fissures in the Western consensus—particularly political actors within their respective traditional allies—to exert political pressure against the moves.

Israel and its supporters will seek to mobilize opposition in the United States and among traditional European allies, while Palestinians and their supporters will seek to mobilize opposition among sympathetic European audiences. Diplomatic positions could quickly become domestic political challenges for countries that partake in an international coalition. Thus, the challenge facing the Western countries would relate not only to creating an inclusive coalition but also to maintaining such a coalition for a reasonable period of time against diplomatic and political challenges.

The ease of reaching a broad consensus of preferred permanent-status outcomes relates to the size and like-mindedness of the coalition behind such an initiative. On this count, a small coalition of like-minded states, while easier to create, could adversely affect the pursuit of peace if seen as lacking all, or a convincing majority of, international stakeholders. Conceptually, creating a coalition of the key stakeholders is not impossible. Not only did such a coalition launch the 1991 Madrid process and the 2003 Roadmap, but the success of the P5+1 in crafting the recent set of agreements with Iran might inspire Western countries and the international community to attempt such an effort in the Palestinian-Israeli conflict.

While this paper looks only into the preferences and policies of Western countries, such countries are likely to solicit at least some Arab participation in building a broader international coalition with impact. Even though much of the Arab world has been in turmoil since late 2011, the 2002 Arab Peace Initiative provides a basis for such participation. By putting forward their own set of ideas for resolving the conflict, and by offering Israel incentives to reach a peace deal, the Arab countries rendered themselves more substantive players in any international attempt to resolve the Palestinian-Israeli conflict. Palestinians have since come to rely more heavily on Arab political support and validation. Within Israel, significant voices, including that of Prime Minister Netanyahu, have increasingly called for a more active role for Arab states. In the last round of negotiations, U.S. secretary of state Kerry recognized this expectation by constantly engaging Arab leaders, including on meaningful issues. Since Western countries have a strong preference that an agreement between Israelis and Palestinians lead to "a comprehensive Arab-Israeli peace" that includes "acceptance of full normal relations with Israel and security for all the states of the region," these Western countries, by pursuing policies that assume an existing on-the-ground situation characterized by two states for two peoples, might create conditions that make it easier for Arab countries to gradually pursue more normal relations with Israel while minimizing the risks, thereby increasing the likelihood not just of a Palestinian-Israeli agreement but also the grand goal of Arab-Israeli peace.

In the absence of an international or even Western coalition, unilateral U.S. parameters could have their own impact by virtue of America's position as the leading international actor in the peace process and the wider region. But by the same token, any U.S. action would raise an additional set of challenges. Namely, any potential U.S. parameters would need to be met with immediate, enthusiastic support from the major international stakeholders, a response that in turn would require a high degree of coordination and prior buy-in from the latter. Notably, the amount of effort needed for such precoordination would approach the effort needed to build a formal international coalition.

A PACKAGE APPROACH

Regardless of whether the alignment of policies with preferences is taken by a broad or narrow coalition, there remains the question of whether countries that do embark on this path implement a package approach that aligns policies with preferences on all four core issues (status, borders, Jerusalem, refugees) or only on one or two issues.

The governments of Sweden, Iceland, and the Vatican have chosen the status issue as the one on which to align their policies with their preferences. Despite the questions this raises on their other policies with respect to borders, Jerusalem, and the displaced persons, refugees, and their descendants, Sweden, Iceland, and the Vatican have refrained, at this point, from aligning their policies with their preferences on these other core issues. Through their action on status, Iceland, Sweden, and the Vatican have clearly demonstrated a preference for one side—the Palestinians. In fact, Sweden has clearly declared that it is acting in this way because it believes the situation is "unequal" and that recognizing Palestine would make it less so. Sweden has thus not only broken rank with the Western position of privileging the negotiations process over outcomes, but it has broken rank even further by privileging one specific outcome to the benefit of one side.

Sweden's pick-and-choose approach can only be justified if indeed the analysis behind it is correct—namely, that the failure of negotiations is due to Israeli strength and that, therefore, strengthening the Palestinian side is key to successful negotiations leading to the desired outcome. The issue then becomes less about aligning policies with preferences and more about strengthening one side against the other in the negotiations process. Since good arguments can also be made that the failure to make peace emerges from the continuous Arab Palestinian denial of the Jewish people's right to self-determination in their ancient homeland and that only Israeli strength can ultimately lead to the abandonment of this denial and therefore to peace, a pick-and-choose policy that strengthens one side against the other could instigate a "diplomatic arms race" whereby each side will seek to convince the Western community that achieving peace requires strengthening its side and weakening the other.

If countries were to align their policies with their preferences to useful effect, *the only coherent and helpful manner in which to proceed is the package approach.* This means that once governments have chosen to align their policies with their preferences, they should do so fully and across all core issues. *Only a package approach would send a clear message that the purpose of aligning Western policies with preferences is to secure the preferred outcome rather than favor either side over the other.* A package approach would mean that Western countries would align all their policies with their preferences regardless of which side would appear to benefit. Such policies would be concerned less with the question of "balance," as Sweden expressed it, and more with whether they are making a future agreement, *as a whole*, more or less likely—that is, whether they are advancing their preferred outcome, even in the absence of a negotiated process: *the countries would then seek to "prejudice" the outcome rather than favor either side.*

HOW ALIGNMENT COULD CONTRIBUTE TO PALESTINIAN-ISRAELI PEACE

Should Western countries choose to fully align their policies with their preferences as a complete package, the implication would be to *fundamentally alter the conditions under which Israelis and Palestinians operate and under which they consider their own policies with respect to the conflict.* Implementation of these policies as a package would most likely produce confusion for both sides, as each would find many of its demands being met but others being denied. Obviously, the sides are likely to laud policies that benefit them and protest those perceived to be to their detriment.

In changing the conditions under which the two

sides consider their own policies, the most important implication of aligning Western policies with preferences would be to substantially reduce the perceived downside and risk for both sides regarding the concessions required to achieve peace based on two states for two peoples. In the past, Western policies have focused on trying to *increase the prospect of an upside* for both sides so that the benefits would outweigh the expected losses and overcome perceived risks. This was also the underlying premise of the Arab Peace Initiative. In parallel, Western countries have been careful not to give the sides any benefits up front, thinking that these are best left as bargaining chips for negotiations. For example, most Western governments have repeatedly tied their full recognition of a state of Palestine to a negotiated agreement with Israel, making this an Israeli bargaining chip and an Israeli concession to be made in negotiations. Alternatively, Western governments have been condoning the indefinite and exponential increase of descendants registered as refugees, thereby reinforcing the "right of return" as a Palestinian bargaining chip and a concession to be made in negotiations.

This means that Western policies to date have served to increase *both* the perceived upside and downside. However, as Daniel Kahneman and Amos Tversky's 1979 paper on prospect theory has demonstrated, humans are far more averse to loss than they are drawn by benefits. In other words, they place greater value on what they stand to lose than on the equivalent benefit and their actions reflect this calculus. This certainly explains the behavior of Israelis and Palestinians over time. Both sides have repeatedly chosen to minimize loss over seeking benefit.

The profound implication of *aligning Western*

policies with preferences would be to operate more in line with prospect theory and the inclinations of the negotiating sides. Western countries would be giving over a large share of the benefits to the sides in advance with no expectation in return—an upside less valuable to the sides than previously perceived. But they would also be taking away the bargaining chips from the sides, thereby substantially limiting the perceived loss, which the sides fear. For example, if all Western countries fully recognize the state of Palestine, directly and in the UN and the Security Council, for Israel to do so would no longer be much of a concession, with the risks and sense of loss in doing so thereby reduced. If Western countries recognize all Palestinians as citizens of Palestine, and no longer as refugees, for Palestinians to concede the "right of return" would not mean much anymore to anyone but themselves, and the risks and sense of loss in doing so could be reduced. The situation following Western countries' implementation of the policy changes could then lead to Israelis and Palestinians having less of an upside in reaching an agreement, but also much less of a downside and far fewer risks.

A NEW INTERNATIONAL PARADIGM?

This paper has examined policy options open to Western countries in the absence of direct Palestinian-Israeli negotiations, designed to maintain the relevance of the two-state solution as a path to peace. It has done so by exploring the gaps between the stated preferences of Western countries and their current policies. It has also argued that the success of such an approach depends to some extent on the existence of a broad Western and even international consensus and, more important, a consistent, simultaneous package approach to all core issues.

The challenge is that these conditions are in part negatively correlated. To begin with, sufficient Western consensus can be achieved by formulating highly general parameters, as in the Roadmap, and by picking and choosing only certain policies, most likely those perceived as least sensitive. However, the more general the principles and less intently the package approach is pursued, the less likely any Western policy will affect the conversation both on the diplomatic and political levels.

Beyond a certain point, the value of expending the political and diplomatic capital necessary to carry through such an initiative is brought into question. Additionally, the parties themselves are prone to strongly argue that excessive vagueness forces them to make potential concessions without concrete gains. Also, if this approach is aimed at moving from a mere statement of preferences to concrete action, then failure to go into some degree of specificity makes it impossible to operationalize policy formulations. It used to be said that "constructive ambiguity" is necessary for making peace between Israel and the Palestinians. After twenty-five years of attempting this approach, such ambiguity appears to be destructive in the Palestinian-Israeli context. What is likely needed in its place is "constructive specificity." But the more specific the policies, the more difficult implementing a package approach and building an international or even Western consensus can be.

The two-state paradigm is indeed under tremendous stress. Opinion polls have consistently indicated a growing sense among both Palestinians and Israelis that while such a solution is desirable, it is unachievable. Uncoordinated and muddled action could add to the confusion surrounding the meaning of a two-state solution. A limited coalition that does not include all major stakeholders would chip at the sense of Western and international consensus over the desired outcome of Palestinian-Israeli peace. An initiative that fails to simultaneously address all core issues and enables individual countries to pick and choose policy choices most convenient and easiest to address could instigate a "diplomatic arms race" rather than make a meaningful contribution to peacemaking.

For the United States in particular, any such initiative must be seen in its wider regional context. Unwillingness to exert the requisite diplomatic and political capital to create an acceptable coalition that would employ a package approach would inevitably raise additional questions about the U.S. willingness or ability to lead in the Middle East. Inability to sustain U.S. commitment to the substance of such an initiative would feed an existing narrative that paints the United States as unwilling to back its positions with effective power and action.

The primary motivator for the advocates of spelling out Western policies and positions regarding permanent-status issues and fully aligning Western policies with these positions is the desire to halt the erosion of the two-state solution. To ensure that such an approach does not hasten the very scenario it aims to prevent, success for the international community under U.S. leadership requires approaching this matter in a clear-eyed way and addressing all permanent-status issues equally, consistently, and simultaneously, with a high degree of specificity, cognizant of the challenges and willing to bear the costs of overcoming them.

EINAT WILF

The Washington Institute for Near East Policy
December 2015

182

V. POSTSCRIPT

The world has an enormous stake in the outcome of the battle for hegemony in the Sunni world in general and the Arab world, in particular. That outcome might determine whether citizens around the world will be safe from attacks on their soil. It might determine whether a new power emerges to threaten Europe, Russia, Africa, Asia and beyond and what kind of Islam will shape the lives of a third of the world's population. Unfortunately, there's little the non-Muslim world could do to shape the result. At most, outside powers might be able to mitigate the worst possible outcomes of the protracted battle for hegemony in the Middle East—and even that's questionable.

The Strategist
May 22, 2017

The Battle for Hegemony in the Middle East

The Game

> The crisis consists precisely in the fact that the old is
> dying and new cannot be born,
> and in this interregnum a great variety of morbid
> symptoms appear.

—Antonio Gramsci, *The prison notebooks*, 1929–1935

The story of the Middle East for decades to come is of a battle for the hegemony of Sunni Islam, especially in the Arab world, and of the efforts by non-Sunni Muslims and non-Muslims to ensure that no dominant Sunni power capable of uniting the Sunni Arab world, and ultimately the Sunni world more broadly, emerges.

The Sunni world in general, and the Arab Sunni world in particular, lies in ruins. In some cases, quite literally. However, the current malaise of the Sunni Arab world shouldn't cover the simple fact that Sunni Muslims make up the majority of Muslims around the world and that the Arab world is almost exclusively Sunni. After the collapse of the Ottoman Empire, due to the intervention of the conquering British and French powers, Sunni Arabs had little to say about their political organisation. Now that they are emerging from a century-long political hiatus, a united Sunni Arab world constitutes one of the biggest, but still contestable, geopolitical prizes.

Whereas borders have been drawn, alliances have been determined and clear regional hegemons have emerged on most of the world's landmass, in the Middle East borders have been erased by the political sandstorm that was the Arab Spring, structures and alliances have been broken and no natural hegemon has yet emerged. Yet, this was a region that was united in the past and therefore has the potential to be united again.

Should a united Sunni Arab polity emerge, especially if it unites under the banner of the more extreme interpretations of Islam, it could constitute an existential threat to the non-Sunni, non-Arab and non-Muslim minorities of the Middle East. Those minorities therefore have no greater strategic imperative than to ensure that no such polity, as well as no hegemonic power capable of creating such a polity, emerges. The defence and diplomatic policies of the minorities of the Middle East should be understood as having been crafted to serve that end.

The policies of the Middle East's non-Sunni and non-Muslim minorities echo the famous description of British foreign policy towards Europe, as put forth in the legendary comedy 'Yes, Minister':

> Britain has had the same foreign policy objective for at least the last 500 years: to create a disunited Europe. In that cause we have fought with the Dutch against the Spanish, with the Germans

against the French, with the French and Italians against the Germans, and with the French against the Germans and Italians.

In the Middle East, the role of Britain in that scenario is played by Iran, Israel and Russia, which, despite their rivalries, all share the consistent goal of a disunited Middle East and are willing to form whatever alliances are necessary to that end.

Sunni actors, for their part, seek to consolidate their position as viable contenders for hegemony of the Sunni world in general and the Sunni Arab world in particular, while at the very least preventing any other serious contender from emerging. Part of becoming a viable contender involves also putting in place domestic policies that help bolster the credibility of the claimant to leadership—be it a state or a non-state actor—among the Sunni Muslims of the region.

Other grand narratives put forward for understanding the Middle East, such as 'the battle between Sunna and Shia Islam', fail to take note of the vast disparity in area and numbers between Sunni and Shia Islam, as well as the near impossibility of Shia Islam dominating the peoples and lands of Sunni Islam. At 10–15%, Shia are the minority in Islam. Outside Iran, Azerbaijan and certain areas of Iraq, they are a beleaguered minority, with Iran as their only protector. This is also the case for Shias in diaspora communities around the world. Shia Islam, as led by Iran, struggles not so much for domination of the Middle East, which a Shia Persian power can hardly expect to achieve, as much as to prevent the emergence of a united Sunni Arab force that would threaten it.

Iran's Islamist revolution of 1979 might have

served to bolster Iran's regional credibility as a Muslim republic, but it also showed that its brand of Islam remains contested and even denied and denigrated in the region. Iran's claim to Islamic leadership can at most be understood as a defence against the notion, frequently promulgated by Sunni Muslims, that it's an illegitimate and heretical nation.

Iran's nuclear policies are also better understood in this light. Iran is not only influenced by the possession of nuclear weapons by Pakistan, but is also a minority power seeking to defend itself against the threat of an emerging hegemon. Iran has walked the fine line between pursuing nuclear capabilities and becoming an actual nuclear weapons power. Walking that fine line has been a carefully crafted policy designed to convey deterrence through the projection of Iran's capacity to develop nuclear weapons, while not going so far as developing weapons that would drive its opponents to also seek full nuclear capabilities that would threaten it in turn.

The Players

The battle to replace the lost hegemony of the Ottoman Empire is waged among those who could credibly claim leadership of the Sunni world over which it once held sway. The serious players in this game are primarily Turkey, Egypt, Saudi Arabia and new Islamist contenders claiming to represent the vision of an Islamic state, or caliphate.

Turkey is the direct heir of the Ottoman Empire and was home to the last accepted caliph, or ruler of the Muslim world. As such, Turkey can make a powerful claim to reuniting the Sunni world under its leadership. However, its development after World War I, in which Ataturk remade it into a modern secular state with a Western orientation, including its disavowal of the role of a caliph, has rendered it for some time an irrelevant player in the game for Sunni dominance. Turkey, like much of the Sunni world that its empire once controlled, is reawakening from its 'lost century' to contest its role as leader of the Sunni world.

As a non-Arab country, Turkey is at a disadvantage as it seeks to unite mostly Sunni Arabs. Erdogan's election and policies—which have solidified Turkey's turn away from the EU and the West towards the Middle East and Caucasus region—have served to slowly remake Turkey into an Islamic country with solid Islamic credentials. To an extent, Erdogan's domestic policies are the Turkish equivalent of Iran's Islamic revolution. However, whereas Iran's Islamic revolution is useful at most to defend Iran against claims of illegitimacy and heresy, which a Shia and Persian country needs to address, Turkey's gradual Islamic revolution, combined with its Ottoman heritage, help to position it as a credible claimant to hegemony over the Sunni world.

Unlike Turkey, **Saudi Arabia** is undeniably both Arab and Islamic. It's the birthplace of Islam and the fountain of the Arab conquests. Saudi Arabia possesses prized assets in the battle for Sunni Arab leadership. They include the sacred cities of Mecca and Medina, its Arabism and of course its control of much of the world's oil reserves and the power to set prices, although that's now weakened by the US. Since the 1970s, Saudi Arabia has successfully used its oil wealth to promote its brand of puritanical Islam—Wahhabism—around the world. In that process, it has changed and even undermined countries from Mauritania to Malaysia, from Ethiopia to Pakistan.

Ostensibly partners of the West in the war on terror,

the Saudis have been called 'both the arsonists and the firefighters'. Under the cover of cultural exchanges and charities, Saudi Arabia has spent an estimated US $75–100 billion exporting extremist ideology by building mosques, publishing textbooks, training imams, establishing TV stations and creating organisations such as the World Muslim League, the World Assembly of Muslim Youth and the International Islamic Relief Organization. A 2005 report estimated that Saudi Arabia spent $120 million inside Australia's Islamic community. Meanwhile, foreign workers who arrive in the kingdom from South Asia return home under the sway of Wahhabism and magnify Saudi Arabia's influence.

Saudi Arabia has a powerful claim to uniting the Arab and Sunni Muslim worlds, as Mohammed and his caliphs did from the seventh to the tenth century. However, it's a fragile country, especially as questions of succession loom large. It has staked the legitimacy of its rule on an alliance with the most fundamentalist form of Islam—a form that has blown back to inspire Islamist contenders such as al-Qaeda and the Islamic State in Iraq and Syria (ISIS) to challenge the legitimacy of the current Saudi regime. Moreover, the Saudis' substantial and visible assets, including their military apparatus and purchases, are a valuable target for any claimant wanting to lead and unite the Sunni Arab world. Islamist non-state actors consider deposing the ruling family a necessary step towards uniting the Sunni Arabs. Saudi Arabia finds itself suspended between laying a claim to leadership and becoming a major battleground among other Sunni forces fighting for hegemony.

The Saudi ruling family faces grave danger from **non-state Islamic contenders** that have made clear their ambitions to unite Sunni Arabs under their leadership. Those contenders, whether al-Qaeda, the intentionally named Islamic State in Iraq and the Levant, or any of the various groups that have been inspired by the Saudis' extremist interpretation of Islam and the notion of separating true believers from heretics, all contend that they have the purest and therefore the best credentials for leading the Sunni Arab world. They also have a clearly stated ambition to do so. In the quest to attain hegemony, they seek to control assets, such as those possessed by Saudi Arabia.

The campaign of terror waged by non-state Islamist groups should be understood as a two-pronged campaign to:

- Position themselves as the only ones committed to an all-out Islamic war against the West
- Delegitimise any other possible contenders for the position of Sunni Arab leadership

By attacking the West, they can more easily portray Saudi Arabia and Egypt as 'in the pocket of the West'. By attacking other non-Sunnis, they bolster their Sunni credentials, and by attacking Sunnis who fail to profess what is according to them the 'one true path' of Islam they set themselves up as the arbiters of faith and heresy in Sunni Islam, delegitimising any contenders as not sufficiently Muslim.

That ISIS is currently the most recognisable face of an Islamist contender for hegemony does not mean that if it's defeated all Islamist contenders are defeated. If that specific Islamic state is defeated, there are others ready to assume the mantle. The working assumption should be that Islamist contenders will be part of the battle for hegemony of the Middle East for decades to come.

Egypt is a perennial claimant to leadership of the Arab world. It certainly views itself as the 'mother of nations' and, given its pre-Arab and pre-Muslim history, the nation that can claim the greatest degree of historical, cultural and national coherence in the region, over millennia. It's also home to the largest number of Sunni Arabs and can therefore make the simple numerical claim to leadership of the Sunni Arab world. Its location between North Africa and the Levant also gives it a geographical advantage.

Under Nasser's pan-Arabism, Egypt appeared close to realising the vision of Arab unity under a secular nationalist ideology. Its crushing defeat by Israel in 1967 (even if partially redeemed by the war of 1973) and its subsequent turn to the West and a peace agreement with Israel have undermined that effort and left Egypt out of the leadership game for several decades, but that doesn't mean that it can't reclaim that position at some point and perhaps succeed more than it did under Nasser.

Currently, Egypt seems more intent on ensuring that no serious rival could emerge, rather than assuming the mantle itself. Even though Egypt is home to one of the most important centres of Islamic learning and interpretation, its Islamic star has been on the wane, the outcome of the staunch secularism of its military rulers, their battles against the Muslim Brotherhood and the success of Saudi Arabia in promoting the Saudi brand of Islamism.

Should Egypt come under a strong and stable Islamist rule, it would become a formidable contender for the Sunni Arab leadership. It might be particularly relevant if Egypt were to reclaim and propagate its relatively more moderate al-Azhar form of Islam and unite the Sunni Arab world under that banner, in opposition to the extremist interpretations in play. However, as long as Egypt lacks powerful Islamist credentials, it's likely to focus on ensuring that, at the very least, no rival claimant to Sunni Arab leadership can emerge.

Egypt's warming relations with Israel under President al-Sisi could be understood in this context. As long as Egypt doesn't work directly to unite the Arab Sunni world, but merely to prevent the emergence of any rival capable of doing that, it will find in Israel a reliable ally who shares that goal and is committed to a disunited Arab Middle East.

Like Iran, **Israel** is a powerful state that's the home of a minority denied and denigrated in the region—the Jews. Whereas Iran is the clear leader and defender of the Shia minority in the region—some of whom don't live in Iran— Israel is the clear leader and defender of the tiny Jewish minority presence in the region. However, unlike Iran, which views itself as protecting Shia minorities throughout the region while also using them for its defence, ever since the Arab and Iranian expulsion of Jews from the region, Israel is the exclusive home of Jews in the region and their defender exclusively within its borders, as almost no Jews exist in the Middle East outside Israel.

Israel and its Jews are threatened, including with potential annihilation, by the spectre of a united Sunni power. In fact, a common view of Israel in the region is that it's a deliberate wedge put in place by the West to prevent a united Sunni power from ever emerging. Israel's position as home to and defender of the Jewish minority also means that it could be relied upon to never compete for hegemony of the Muslim and Arab world. This makes Israel, as long as it remains powerful, a potential 'joker' ally to be used by the various players in the grand battle to ensure that none of their rivals emerges as a hegemon.

While this grand struggle might appear to be contained to the region of the Middle East and North Africa, its development has profound implications for Russia, Africa, Asia and the West. The simple reason is that whenever Islam was united, whether under Arab or Ottoman rule, it attacked and conquered large parts of Europe, Africa and Asia. A united Sunni world is an expanding one. In Islamic history, as in the history of all civilisations, expansion and conquest follow in the wake of unification.

One look at the map of the global distribution of Sunni Islam and the **Russian** geopolitical imperative becomes crystal clear: prevent the emergence of any serious contender for a united Sunni leadership. The danger of a powerful united Islam on its borders, uniting Central Asia, with its wealth of natural resources, is the definition of a Russian nightmare. Russia, like Iran and like Israel, wants a disunited Middle East.

There are those who are tempted to view Russia's intervention in the Middle East, especially in Syria, as heralding a new Cold War. There's no doubt that Putin takes a certain pleasure in exposing American weakness and hesitancy, but Russia's position in the Middle East is that of a regional divider, not a global uniter. Russia, like Israel and like Iran, can't unite the Sunni world under its banner. Even if it were to cast itself in the role of protector of the region's Christians, it would be nearly unemployed, as Christians are fast disappearing from the region through war, exodus, ethnic cleansing and genocide.

Russia's interests in the Middle East, then, aren't ones of global hegemony, but of the defence of its interests in a neighbourhood that threatens its very core. Since Russia, as an Orthodox Christian nation, can make no credible claim for hegemony in the Muslim Middle East, it serves as a useful ally for those, such as Iran and Israel, that share its goal of a permanently disunited Middle East. It's also a useful ally for potential contenders for hegemony, such as Turkey, Saudi Arabia and Egypt, which it can aid in preventing their rivals from rising above them.

Ironically, the one player in the Middle East that remains a mystery is the **United States**. Whereas all the other actors—including Russia—are of the region and therefore have specific and clear interests that relate to their very existence, defence and power, the interests of the US in the region remain unclear, probably also to itself.

The US can theoretically choose to leave behind the region and pivot to Asia—a choice unavailable to all the other actors, who are of the region and in the region. Other than a general desire to prevent terrorism from reaching US soil, it's no longer clear whether the US has clear interests in the region that it's committed to protect. With technological advances in energy, it's no longer clear even whether the US has economic and energy interests in the region. And, if it doesn't, is there anything else to keep it involved?

It's not clear whether the US favours a united or a disunited Middle East and whether it has a position on the matter at all. Washington clearly wants a less bothersome Middle East, but it's not clear what it's willing to do to achieve that end. While President Trump speaks of standing by the US's traditional allies in the Middle East, especially Israel and Saudi Arabia, the US continues to project a lack of clarity about its interests and commitments in the region. This has already led all the other players to operate under the assumption of substantially decreased US presence and commitment, until events prove otherwise.

The Battleground Theaters

In the grand strategic game of the Middle East—defined here as the battle to lead or thwart Sunni, and especially Sunni Arab, unification and hegemony—the players are grouped into those capable of leading (Turkey, Egypt, Saudi, Islamist contenders) or thwarting (Iran, Israel, Russia). The board on which they are playing the game includes four major ongoing battlegrounds (**Syria, Iraq, Libya, Yemen**) and five or six potential battlegrounds (**Lebanon, Jordan, Saudi Arabia**, the various **Gulf states, Egypt**, perhaps **Turkey**). Algeria, Tunisia and Morocco are likely to remain at the margins but will be profoundly affected by the outcomes of the other battles.

Saudi Arabia, Egypt and Turkey are notable for being both potential leaders of the Muslim Sunni world and potential battlegrounds in the struggle to dominate that world.

Syria and Iraq are the central theatre, where the main battle is taking place. All the relevant actors are present in one form or another: Iran, Russia, Turkey, Saudi Arabia, the Gulf states and various Islamist contenders, with Egypt and Israel at the margins. While Syria lacks valuable natural resources and centres of Islamic legitimacy, it's a historical centre of Islamic rule, and its territory, together with the Sunni part of Iraq, forms the second population pole of the Sunni Arab world (with Egypt as the second pole).

The territories of Iraq are reminiscent of the German-speaking territories in Europe in the mid-19th century: a grand mass in the centre of a region in turmoil, up for grabs by those who can unite them. The similarity also extends, as happened several decades after German unification, to the possibility of a unification under an extremist ideology that's then used as a basis for conquering and uniting the entire region under its banner.

The various actors in the region understand that, just as a united Nazi Germany was well placed to begin a campaign of conquest across Europe, threatening at its peak the Soviet Union, Britain, North Africa and the Middle East, whichever actor succeeds in uniting the Sunni Arab parts of Iraq and Syria would be well placed to further unite the Arab world. It could move from the territories of Iraq and Syria into Lebanon and Jordan and perhaps Palestine (the rest of the Levant alluded to in the Islamic State's name), into the grand prize of Saudi Arabia and the Gulf states, with their wealth and advanced military equipment, and from there into North Africa, Turkey, the Caucasus, Europe and Russia.

Russia, Iran, Turkey, Saudi Arabia and the Gulf states understand that if the unification were to take place under the extremist ideology of the various Islamist contenders, be it the Islamic State or a new incarnation, it poses an immediate danger of annihilation to all who fall outside the purview of its version of Islam, which means Jews, Christians and Shias, as well as all Sunnis who would refuse to submit. The ferocity with which the war's being fought is a consequence of the understanding shared by all actors that the battle for Syria isn't merely about drawing borders and dividing territory, but an existential battle that could determine the future existence of various peoples of the region. America's choice, a single attack aside, to stay away from Syria and to engage in very limited fighting against the Islamic State (just as it did for the European theatre throughout much of World War II) reflects its assessment that it's still very far away from being threatened by the outcomes of that war.

The Syrian and Iraqi battles are threatening to turn neighbouring areas into new battlegrounds. The flows of refugees from Syria and Iraq into Jordan and Lebanon further threaten those already very fragile countries. It's certainly the intention of the Islamist contenders that all of the Levant, which includes Lebanon, Jordan, Israel and Palestine, should come under their rule. Cognisant of the dangerous possibility of becoming battlegrounds, the leaderships and populations of Jordan and Lebanon are struggling to manoeuvre carefully, and have so far avoided the worst manifestations of the revolutionary fervour of the early Arab Spring. However, the fragility of both countries is apparent, and scenarios in which they become battlegrounds in the game should be seriously considered.

Beyond Jordan lies the grand prize of Saudi Arabia and the Gulf states, which the Islamist contenders seek to rule. The fall of Saudi Arabia into the hands of a non-state extremist Islamist group is a scenario that needs to be seriously considered, if for no other reason than that it's the declared goal of all of those groups. Ironically, if such an organisation were to take over Saudi Arabia, it would be the place where the Islamists would have to make the least adjustments to law and society to bring them into line with the most extreme interpretation of Islamic law. Precisely because Saudi Arabia and the Gulf states possess the ultimate prizes for all those would seek Middle Eastern hegemony (Mecca, Medina, much of the world's oil and large caches of advanced military equipment), the fall of the Saudi ruling family, or any other sign that Saudi Arabia is turning from contender to battleground, would be likely to spark even greater involvement in the battle, including by the US.

The battle for Yemen could be understood as being fought in the shadow of that possibility. Yemen is a nearly failed country that's the geographical, social and political Achilles' heel of the Arabian Peninsula. Any struggle for hegemony is likely to involve it as a southern gateway to Saudi Arabia. It's no accident that the last wave of efforts at Arab unification under Nasser involved another murderous war in Yemen. Whereas Islamist contenders are using it to get to Saudi Arabia from the south, the Saudis are fighting bitterly in Yemen to protect their flank. Iran is also involved in the war, with the twin goals of protecting Yemen's Shia minority and thwarting Saudi Arabia's and other Islamist contenders' attempts to unify the Arabian Peninsula.

In North Africa, for the moment, Libya is the only active battleground. Since the various battles taking place in its territory are between competing tribes, the war remains relatively contained, and the various actors in this latest grand game for hegemony have chosen not to intervene in any substantial way. Libya is mostly a battleground for various forms of Islamism, and all actors in the region are keeping a wary eye on it to see whether anything develops that threatens the region more broadly. For now, Morocco, Tunisia and Algeria are successfully working to contain the Libyan battle, but should they fail they face a danger of becoming, at the minimum, ideological battlegrounds for Islamism.

Egypt was briefly a battleground for Islamism. The battle is now suspended, but the millions of Egyptians who voted for the Muslim Brotherhood in 2012 haven't disappeared simply because a military coup reversed the election results. How long the military could fend off the rise of an Islamist Egypt remains in question, and the polity is still fragile. Egypt's geography, population and cultural cohesion mean that it's unlikely to be broken apart like Syria or Iraq, but the domestic battle for an Islamist Egypt is likely to erupt again in the future. It might not involve any clear outside intervention, as in the case of Iraq, but the actors in the region will have a major stake in whether Egypt turns Islamist and, if it does, under what brand of Islamism.

The Tools of the Game

With the game, players and battlegrounds defined, the ability of the players to achieve their aims depends on the tools at their disposal and whether they make effective use of them. In terms of the traditional tools of power—territory, people, military and economic resources—the various actors differ, and none emerges as the absolute clear hegemon. There's no natural hegemon to the Sunni world, or to the Sunni Arab world, as exists in other regions of the world. There's no single country that can make a credible claim to uniting the Sunni Arab world that also enjoys a preponderance of power in all its various forms. This means that not only is the struggle for hegemony likely to be drawn out over decades, if not longer, but also that the ability of the various actors to be effective and have an edge depends on their sophisticated use of other forms of power, such as so-called 'soft' power.

In the Middle East, soft power is found in the form of appeals of loyalty to religion, sect, ethnicity, tribe and nation as well as the ability to forge ever-shifting alliances in the service of specific goals. To put these various forms of power to effective use, the region's leaders, rulers and political actors require a level of sophistication that was once associated with the great Metternich.

One of the reasons that the Middle East seems to confound so many outside, and especially Western, observers is that various forms of deadly loyalties to a collective—whether it's a tribe, a religious sect or a nation—seem to exert power that many in the West consider to be long gone, or at least that should be long gone. In that sense, the 'soft' power isn't so at all. In the intellectual centres of the West, the prevailing 21st century ideology is universalist and refuses to acknowledge fealty to anything less general than the human race (for some, even that's too parochial, and one must care about all living things equally). The idea that humans would fight, kill and be killed for a subsection of humanity to which they are loyal above others—whether it's called a tribe, a sect or a nation—is considered abhorrent to the universalist mindset, which is prevalent among many policymakers in the West.

Yet, not so long ago, in the West's own core, Yugoslavia blew up in a murderous civil war when the pressure-cooker lid of Tito's autocratic rule was lifted. Neighbours and family members slaughtered each other in the name of loyalties supposedly long forgotten. Modern Europeans who thought they had put their own ethnic and national butchery behind them watched in horror how century-old loyalties and rivalries proved far more powerful than the modern Yugoslavian identity. Yugoslavia was just the tail end of several centuries in which the European continent was engulfed in ongoing murderous battles between competing loyalties to kings and princes, nations and empires. The modern and peaceful structure of Europe could only emerge once the bloody battle between all the competing loyalties was spent.

While Europe might yet find that it hasn't put its past completely behind it, in much of the world, especially in times of chaos, family, tribe, sect, nation and religion remain remarkably powerful as a source of order, meaning and solidarity. They are able to lay claim to the allegiance of the individual and inspire acts of terror and sacrifice that no other forms of power could. Therefore, those who can command people's loyalties and willingness to fight and sacrifice through an appeal to their sense of protecting 'us against them' are likely to command greater power than is apparent by a simple accounting of people, economies and armies.

In fact, these forms of allegiance and loyalty are so powerful that they also transcend any accounting of territory and borders. Especially with zero-cost international communications, social media and low-cost flights, people can express a sense of belonging to a tribe, sect, nation and religion across the globe. They can be inspired to take extreme actions and even sacrifice their lives on behalf of those loyalties while living halfway across the world from their territorial centre.

The religion of **Islam** remains the most powerful force in the grand game for the Middle East. The battle for hegemony is waged first and foremost in the world of Islam. Islam recognises no central authority and, as a religion of written and oral law, it's in the hands of its interpreters. Those who can compel the greatest number of followers to their interpretation of Islam wield a powerful weapon in the battle for hegemony.

The ability to make an appeal to the broad mass of Sunnis across the Middle East and beyond is a critical factor in determining the outcome of the battle for hegemony. This battle is fought in all manners, from religious pronouncements, to theological conferences, to social media and terrorism and, of course, to the funding of certain groups. The kind of Islam that ultimately triumphs is of interest not just to the region but to the Islamic world more broadly and the rest of the world where Muslim minorities live. There's no determinism in this battle. The triumph of Wahhabism across the Middle East is by no means guaranteed for the long term; it's also as likely to create backlash. The vast majority of Muslims don't belong to that school of thought and don't subscribe to the idea that violent beliefs and actions are the way of Islam. This creates room for countries such as Egypt, Jordan, Tunisia and Morocco to appeal at one point to those seeking to free themselves from the temptations of fundamentalism.

While Islam encompasses the entire region, among the region's people, predating Islam and still remarkably powerful, especially in certain areas, is the appeal to the **tribe**. Tribal loyalty and belonging is the oldest recorded form of political, social and judicial organisation. The Middle East and Africa remain the places in the world where that identity is most powerful and present in many people's lives. The battle for hegemony in the region depends on the ability to appeal to tribal loyalties and to create coalitions and alliances that bring together previously warring tribes. As more territories become contested battlegrounds, loyalty to the tribe is likely to become an ever more powerful currency in the battle.

During the century from the fall of the Ottoman Empire to the Arab Spring, when 'old' religious, sectarian, ethnic and tribal loyalties were being laid low in a Middle East carved up by the victorious powers, new loyalties to new nations were being forged. Those loyalties, despite their 'newness', can't be written off easily. By now, they have been in play for nearly a century. People across the Middle East have grown up as Syrians, Iraqis, Jordanians or Saudis. That has power. The new loyalties also have the power of interests: powerful economic and military interests are tied to keeping them alive. The disintegration of Syria is also proving that keeping the new loyalties from succumbing to the old ones is the one thing that stands between a nation's people and complete chaos. An appeal to the unity of the nation against the danger of chaos might be the only thing keeping countries such as Lebanon and Jordan from turning into the bloody battleground that is Syria.

Between the new and old loyalties lie the minorities of the Middle East, who themselves become a tool in the battle for hegemony. The ability to appeal to the religious, sectarian, ethnic and tribal loyalties of the minorities to undermine whatever national loyalty they might have is another not-so-soft tool of power that the various players have at their disposal. The minorities in play include the Kurds in Turkey, Iran, Iraq and Syria; outside Iran, the Shias in Iraq, Saudi Arabia, Yemen, Syria, Lebanon and the Gulf states; in Egypt, the Coptic Christians.

Beyond the region, Muslim minorities in Russia and across the world are a critical element in the game for regional hegemony. Iran defends itself and creates deterrence by casting its protection over the Shia minorities of the region. The Kurds use their ethnic loyalty and are being used to undermine the countries where they have a significant presence. And the Islamic State uses Muslim minorities around the world to undermine the West and increase its credibility as a claimant to the leadership of the

Sunni Arab world.

The multiplicity of actors and loyalties in the grand game of the Middle East means that the ability to forge alliances within and across these loyalties remains the most important skill required of the leaders in the region. In the absence of a clear and natural hegemon, the ability of any claimant to rise to hegemony will depend on the strength and quality of their alliances, and the same holds true for those seeking to thwart the rise of any hegemon. Yet, these alliances are likely to be written in the sand. Any effort to define an 'axis' is likely to fall prey to the players' ever-shifting interests. Whatever axes of alliances appear at any given moment, they are temporary arrangements until a more stable regional order emerges. There's little use trying to analyse them as permanent structures.

Exacerbating Factors

Whereas the basic conditions of the battle for hegemony seem already to presage a long and drawn-out battle, outside factors worsen even that grim outlook. First and foremost among those factors is the **youth bulge** being experienced across the Muslim world. A youth bulge occurs when advances in medicine lead to a marked drop in infant mortality but social norms still favour high birthrates. When societies experience rapid economic growth, youth bulges can contribute to economic prosperity as the young people enter an expanding work force. However, if the economy fails to create new and productive jobs to meet the growth in population, the masses of young people, and especially young men, tend to gravitate to social unrest, revolution and war. Youth bulges are now considered to have been major factors contributing to the intensity of the French Revolution, World War I, World War II and social unrest in Latin

America in the 1970s and 1980s.

There's no question that the Muslim and Arab worlds are experiencing a youth bulge. According to a 2015 Pew Research Center study, the number of Muslims worldwide is expected to grow by 73% from 2010 to 2050, and Muslims are expected to outnumber Christians by 2070.

There's also no question that economic prospects are grim across the Sunni Arab world. Economies are mismanaged or, rather, managed for the benefit of the few, are over-dependent on oil, or are devastated by war. The conditions for economic growth, whether they are quality education, innovation or open societies, are largely absent. Barring a miracle, the youth bulge will spell only disaster for the Arab and Muslim world. The various contenders for hegemony should be able to draw on a nearly limitless pool of disaffected young men to engage in protracted butchery.

The one natural resource that was able to shield the Sunni Arab world from responsible governance has lost its status as a cure-all-ills commodity. For decades, as rentier states, many countries in the Arab world, especially those in the Gulf, relied on massive oil and gas exports to bankroll a functioning state and economy. **Oil and gas** account for more than 50% of GDP among the Arab states that are members of the Organization of Petroleum Exporting Countries. Oil revenues were essentially used to run a centralised welfare state and buy political stability.

With energy sales inflating economic growth over the past two decades, oil-rich governments avoided economic liberalisation and diversification. Rather than creating other drivers of economic growth and shielding themselves from the possibility of oil losing its financial and strategic value, the Gulf states preferred to control the price of oil by setting production limits, ensuring that their resources lasted several generations, while investing in sovereign wealth funds and foreign asset reserves to build up financial reserves. The assumption in their strategy was that oil would remain a strategic commodity and they would continue to hold the reins of its price and production. But the rug is starting to be removed from under their feet.

A number of factors have contributed to economic trouble among the oil-exporting Arab states. As their populations expanded at the highest growth rate in the world over the past decade, which required enlarged government budgets to expand their welfare states and make up for rampant unemployment, their oil revenues dropped significantly. Starting in mid-2014, even amid conflict in the Middle East (which usually causes a spike in oil prices), the price of oil began to fall dramatically as a result of economic turmoil in Europe and Asia, energy efficiency, and increased US oil production. The drop in prices has caused the Gulf states to dip into their financial reserves to make up for their increased budgets and decreased revenues.

The political turmoil that has unfolded in the region, especially the Islamic State taking control (and subsequently losing) large oil fields in Iraq and Syria, which it used to finance its operations, combined with the lower price of oil, has contributed to a significant decrease in foreign direct investment flowing into Arab states, further slowing economic growth. If these trends continue and the oil-exporting Arab states spend their wealth funds and foreign currency reserves making up for budget deficits, eventually their funds will run out and the economic situation could become catastrophic.

The Middle East and North Africa are also plagued by an **environmental crisis** that could prove to be more disastrous than armed conflict. The region's extremely dry climate, growing population, pollution, poorly managed water resources and susceptibility to the effects of climate change will cause severe water scarcity and pose an existential threat. Some even argue that the devastating drought in Syria from 2006 to 2011 contributed to social unrest that evolved into civil war.

According to the World Bank, in 1962 the Arab world had 1,335 cubic metres of fresh water per capita; as of 2014, that volume had dwindled to around 295 cubic metres (the world average in 2014 was 5,925 cubic metres). Global warming is causing temperatures to rise, which corresponds to a decline in rainfall and thus further reduces the availability of fresh water and causes desertification. The UN's Intergovernmental Panel on Climate Change estimates that 60% of Syria faces desertification; Iraq faces desertification at a rate of 0.5% per year; in Jordan, it's estimated that as much as 30% of the country's surface water resources has been lost due to drought and desertification. The flow in the Euphrates is expected to decline by 50% by 2025, which would lead to an estimated shortage of 33 billion cubic metres of water per year.

The environmental conditions alone make it a difficult challenge for the most developed nations to provide sustainable water resources, yet the region will need to find solutions to supply water to a thirsty population amidst regional chaos and conflict. But water scarcity only adds to the regional turmoil (when it isn't the cause of the turmoil), as most of the water resources are transboundary: the Jordan River is a water source for

Lebanon, Syria, Israel, Jordan and the Palestinian Territories; the Yarmouk River is shared by Syria and Jordan; the Disi aquifer runs along the border of Jordan and Saudi Arabia; the Euphrates River flows through Turkey, Syria, Iraq and Iran.

Summary

In the years following 9/11, the UN published a series of *Arab development reports*. The 2009 report, focused on human security, concluded that human insecurity was pervasive in the Arab world and noted that external threats such as pollution, terrorism, migration, pandemics and drug and human trafficking have challenged state security, while growing poverty, civil wars, ethnic and sectarian conflicts and authoritarian regimes were limiting the rights and freedoms of Arab citizens. Since the report was published, the situation has become much worse. The Arab Spring turned to winter, hundreds of thousands of people have been killed and millions more have become refugees or internally displaced, while none of the underlying problems of the Arab world, from gender inequality to stunted development, is showing any signs of improvement.

The world has an enormous stake in the outcome of the battle for hegemony in the Sunni world in general and the Arab world, in particular. That outcome might determine whether citizens around the world will be safe from attacks on their soil. It might determine whether a new power emerges to threaten Europe, Russia, Africa, Asia and beyond and what kind of Islam will shape the lives of a third of the world's population. Unfortunately, there's little the non-Muslim world could do to shape the result. At most, outside powers might be able to mitigate the worst possible outcomes of the protracted battle for hegemony in the Middle East—and even that's questionable.

Outside observers of the Middle East should realise that, for the first time in a century, what's happening across the Sunni Arab world is authentic, but that 'authentic' doesn't necessarily mean positive. It only means that what's happening is an authentic expression of the various pressures and powers of the Sunni Arabs themselves. Ultimately, the Sunnis in general and the Sunni Arabs in particular will have to work out their regional order for themselves. This is a process that will take time—decades, perhaps a century—and can't be condensed or accelerated. No outside power can do it for them. Either a clear hegemon will emerge or the various sides will spend themselves in battles to the point of exhaustion, leading perhaps to a balanced compromise.

Whatever regional order emerges, it will have to be described in terms that come from Islamic, Sunni and Arab history. Islam is a political religion that has clear conceptions of the proper world order and the way public and private matters should be ruled and arranged. Whatever regional order emerges, whoever the hegemon, it will be rooted in Islam as the cultural language of the region. The idea of the caliphate isn't going away. It's merely the historical Islamic form of Arab and Muslim unity—a fundamental political organising principle. Even if the current organisation that goes by the name of the Islamic State is defeated, the idea of an Islamic state will continue to hold sway as the organising principle of the Sunni Arab world and the Muslim world more broadly.

One can compare the idea of the caliphate and the Islamic state to the idea of a unified European continent.

That idea has an old lineage, and it served not only Napoleon and Hitler but also Jean Monnet, a founder of the European Union. An Islamic state, a caliphate and a united Sunni Arab world need not in themselves threaten the world at large, but under a certain interpretation of Islam they pose a threat.

The Strategist
May 22, 2017